SECOND CHANCE
at a GREAT
RELATIONSHIP

SECOND CHANCE
at a GREAT
RELATIONSHIP

Let Go Of

The Resentment,

Return To Love

DR. DEAN DORMAN

PRINCIPIA
MEDIA

It's not your communication skills that need improvement: it's your ability to finish your arguments that needs to improve

- Learn why most people fall out of love (and more importantly how they can fall back in love by applying some simple techniques)
- Understand the role that frequent unresolved arguments play in breaking down the sense of connectedness in a relationship.
- Identify the role that each individual plays in the resentment dynamic and how to break these cycles.

You Need This Book If:

- You and your spouse have frequent arguments, most of which are left unresolved.
- You feel emotionally alienated from your mate.
- Arguments are more hurtful than productive and include swearing, name-calling, harsh words, and accusations.
- Your marriage brings you no joy and you cringe at the thought of spending time with your mate.
- You have difficulty talking to your mate without the conversation ending up in a fight.

"The grass isn't greener on the other side of the fence. Grass is greener where you water it."

—Michael Ceo

"Love is that condition in which the happiness of another person is essential to your own."

—Robert Heinlein, *Stranger in a Strange Land*

How We Fall Out of Love:

- When we find someone especially attractive, our brains produce neurotransmitters. These brain chemicals make us feel like we are "high." We feel infatuation (but we think we are in love.)

- We don't really fall in love with our love interest, but rather their "representative" or that part of them they want us to see. If left uninterrupted by reality, we start to have feelings for our lover. But the neurotransmitters of love blind us to the true nature of our love interest.

- If the person that we have these feelings for is at least 80 percent of the person they passed themselves off as being, there is little, if any, resentment. If not, there tends to be a sense of disconnection and betrayal once the neurotransmitters wear off (about a year). This means that there can be a sense of "what happened to the guy/girl I fell in love with."

- We will do almost anything to continue the delivery of these brain chemicals. These chemicals are very powerful, so powerful that they trump even our natural tendencies. If we are private, we become talkative; if we are depressed, we become happy; if we are lazy, we have boundless energy. With time, we move from infatuation to real love, the neurotransmitters of love are replaced by other brain chemicals that make us feel comfortable or relaxed when we are with our partner. (We no longer feel the pitter-patter in our hearts.)

- We marry, we have children, and we go on with life. Naturally there are issues that we have to resolve. Issues like parenting, sex, chores, spending…

- If we have the ability to argue constructively and "stay in the ring," we resolve our issues without too much resentment being generated. If we can't resolve our issues, however, if our partners call us names, interrupt us, bring up stuff from the past, or threaten to leave us, what happens to the issue? What happens is we don't resolve the issue, *because our arguments get derailed.*
- When issues are left unresolved they don't go away. We open up the basement door and kick them down in the basement. They build up and become resentment. When the resentment builds up to a critical mass, we start to disconnect emotionally.
- When we disconnect emotionally we no longer feel like our partner is filling our cup emotionally. When this happens we look for things in our lives that *do fill our cup.* We start to focus on things like our careers, our children, shopping, friends, and hobbies, but these things push us farther away from our partner, not closer.
- When we feel that the trust and respect for our partners begins to wane, we start to ask ourselves, "How much of my heart should I be holding back? How much am I willing to be hurt if this does not work out?" This does not necessarily mean we are leaving, but it may mean we fantasize about it or start to make plans... just in case.
- We start to become guarded and not allow our partner into our inner world. The very things that drew us to our mate, *the laughing, joking, playing, sex, and talking dry up, and we feel like roommates.* We feel emotionally disconnected.

TABLE OF CONTENTS

INTRODUCTION

A better relationship with our partner is a journey as much as it is a destination. It's a process, not an insight. This book should be read not as a novel, but as a series of insights. Take the ones you like or that pertain to you and discard the rest. You don't have to agree with everything I say, and, frankly, I wouldn't expect you to. The subject that I discuss here is broad and there is no way to explain each and every dynamic and situation that can occur in a marriage. However, this book contains 20 years of my experience as a psychologist and marriage counselor, and I know that those insights have helped thousands of couples to have a more satisfying and fulfilling relationship.

Some long-term relationships are successful on their first attempt. Usually this couple is such a good match that there are very few things for them to argue about or they have the tools in their toolbox to resolve what differences they do have. This is certainly the exception, not the rule however. The reality is that many relationships need a second chance to attain the type of relationship they really seek. A relationship that leaves them emotionally satisfied, trusting of their partner, and with the security to allow their partner into their inner world. As I have said, sometimes individuals have the skills to maintain a good relationship, but sometimes they have to learn those skills.

This book is about learning the skills to develop and maintain a great relationship; the skills to understand the issues that generate resentments and the ability to tolerate the discomfort of discussing uncomfortable topics with your partner. In essence it is a book designed to give you the skills to have a second chance at a great relationship.

Something has happened to marriage in the United States. With divorce rates ranging from 50 to 60 percent, it is no wonder that people cringe when they hear someone they love is "getting married." With the changing role of the family and women no longer willing to live in "classic 50s marriages," the role of marriage started to change. This, coupled with the throwaway culture that was established in the early seventies, started a trend. Couples started to divorce and start over with a different mate; rather than fix their broken relationship. Often what I find is that the couple is not a particularly bad match. In fact, most report that they were happy for years until some incident triggered a resentment dynamic which ultimately lead to an increase in resentment and, eventually, to a sense of being disconnected emotionally. Perhaps the reason I still believe in marriage is that I am actually very successful at improving marriages which are dying. In fact, my strategy is successful in saving the marriages of 90 percent of the couples that come to me for help. *And I can save yours.*

My experience is that almost everyone I treat has a desire to be in a relationship that leaves him or her feeling emotionally connected, happy, sexually satisfied, and contented. People want to be known so well by another that they can almost anticipate their wants; essentially to be in a relationship with someone that "gets them." Developing this type of relationship and being able to maintain this type of relationship are two different things. What I have discovered over the course of doing marriage counseling for over twenty years is that decreasing resentments and learning how to resolve disagreements once and for all is the key to maintaining and improving your relationship. Using my simple approaches, you can learn how to identify what is causing you to feel resentment toward your partner and (more importantly) how to "stay in the ring" to resolve your differences. This will leave you feeling more emotionally connected and, ultimately, back in love.

Rather than going along with the trend of simply leaving your mate and starting over, hoping for a different outcome, why not try some of the simple strategies I suggest in my approach? Why not try and polish your current relationship before starting over with another. In the majority of cases, unless each of you learn to resolve your arguments and keep the resentment to a minimum, the same outcome, essentially growing apart and feeling like roommates, is bound to happen again in your next relationship. If I have learned anything over twenty years, it's that getting rid of your partner does not guarantee that you will get rid of the problem.

Chapter One

GETTING STARTED

What happens when people fall in love? It's important to keep in mind that falling in love is not the same thing as falling into infatuation. Infatuation is a chemical process creating a drug-like state. When we become infatuated, our brains produce neurotransmitters, or chemicals, that I call 'neurotransmitters of love.' These chemicals make us feel good. In fact, they make us feel high. So high, that we have blinders on regarding the focus of our infatuation. We are, in essence, blinded by our love. This is not true love of course.

True love takes time to develop and mature. Infatuation is a sense of being intoxicated by the very presence or thought of our love interest. The problem with infatuation is that it has chemical-like effects. And as with any chemical that can make us high, we can become addicted to it. The chemicals that are known to be associated with the infatuation process are naturally occurring substances known as PEA and the neurotransmitter dopamine. They act together much like a natural amphetamine. When released in our brains, we feel happy, we have boundless energy, and we could stay up all night talking to our love interest.

These chemicals are extremely powerful, however. So powerful, in fact, that they can 'trump' a person's normal emotional status. For a period of time, (frequently a year-and-a-half to three years), the effects of these neurotransmitters will influence the individual's personality. For example: if an individual is depressed, they will frequently feel happy. If they have low levels of energy, they frequently have boundless energy. If they are shy, they frequently become outgoing and talkative. If their natural tendency is to be perfectionistic, they will frequently become tolerant of many things the other does. Individuals who normally have low interest in sex may, for a period, become extremely passionate and interested in physical intimacy.

These short-term changes in personality can lead to misconceptions later. The individual who feels attraction may mistakenly believe that what they have found is someone that is happy, smiling, and easy going; someone who is talkative, energetic, and willing to open up about their inner world; someone who likes to have sex. This condition may stick around. More likely, is that reality sneaks back and after the neurotransmitters of love wear off, the default personality mode returns to the surface. In a large portion of relationships, once a person returns to their prior state, there is a huge disconnection between what their partner thought they were getting and what they actually got.

What I typically see is that for one to three years, their partner was happy, healthy, talkative, and energetic; then they reverted back to being sullen, unhappy, irritable, untalkative, or perfectionistic. This can be confusing for the person they fell in love with. They ask, what happened to my wife or girlfriend? What happened to the guy I fell in love with?

There can be a second by-product of this release of neurotransmitters. If an individual has historically been depressed but when in love felt normal or happy, they can become addicted to those chemicals that were responsible for this chemically produced happiness. This means that once they fall out of the state of infatuation and return to their normal mood, they can go through withdrawal and wish to return to their prior state. Their lovers no longer elicit this response. This means that some individuals chase the feeling they once had by seeking *another* relationship. One that will once again make them feel the way they did in the past; happy, carefree, and normal.

Once the neurotransmitters of love wear off, what is revealed is the real person that you have bonded with. In essence, the blinders of love have been taken off. If what is revealed is reasonably close to the person you thought you were getting, there tends to be little resentment or frustration. If the difference between what you thought you were getting and the actual partner you end up with is significantly different, this can form the initial foundation for resentments, or more significantly, the beginnings of a resentment dynamic.

The neurotransmitters of love and the process of finding out what you are going to end up with (as opposed to what you thought you were going to get in a partner), is only the first wave of threats to long-term monogamous relationships. There are other hurdles: adding children to the equation, careers, boredom, and the building up of a critical mass of resentment over time.

The Role of Resentment in Breaking Down Connectedness

What is the difference between a happy couple and an unhappy couple, between couples that have been married for years yet remain emotionally connected versus couples that feel more like roommates? Each of these couples has the same issues to resolve, the same chores, the same money problems, and the same parenting dilemmas. The key, I have found after doing couples counseling for over twenty years is this: happy couples have found a way to **resolve their arguments**. When you can't find a way to resolve your arguments, the resentments build up and the sense of emotional connection and intimacy deteriorates.

Clients don't come to therapy to learn to resolve their differences. They come to discuss their communication skills, argue over who spent the most money, and who did the fewest chores. Regardless of why couples initially come to counseling, what I found in 80 percent of the marriages I was treating was that underneath the presenting problem laid a similar problem. The underlying problem was the same: arguments that were left unresolved. The metaphor I use is "getting in the ring." Some couples can get in the ring and stay in the ring, and some couples have a hard time getting in the ring and an even harder time staying in the ring.

Getting in the ring means that dreaded arena where couples argue and in most cases undo whatever healing has taken place since the last argument. Using hurtful words and disrespectful tones, they enter the field of battle to fight the one they love the most. Disagreements are inevitable in long-term relationships. There will always be the need for mid-course corrections. What keeps couples from staying in the ring? What derailed the argument and kept them from maintaining the discussion until it was resolved? This inability to stay in the ring is usually due to one of two reasons.

First, when arguments became too uncomfortable, one or both individuals leave or get out of the ring. The second most common reason for lack of resolution is the use of a strategy that a person had learned to use in the past; a strategy that worked in the short run but never in the long run. This usually meant the use of strategies like name calling, pointing fingers, bringing up things from the past, or interrupting.

The reason that arguments become too uncomfortable varies greatly and we will go into more detail later. For most, it is as simple as one or both parties using disrespectful tones of voice or one of the parties crying or doing some type of guilt induction. Sometimes it is as simple as being uncomfortable because someone broke one or more of your unstated rules. Name calling and swearing come into play in a good portion of the arguments, as do getting into the other's personal space, and going down every path other than the one leading to resolution. There are literally hundreds more; many I will discuss in detail later. Each couple is different and has their own typical argument.

It is important to identify why the couple gets out of the ring. More importantly we need to discover why arguments make these individuals feel uncomfortable to begin with. Most people don't like conflict. Many were taught as a good citizen in society that conflict is bad and to love one another. However, there is a difference between conflict that makes one feel uncomfortable and conflict avoidance, (or simply fleeing from arguments).

It is important to help couples learn what early experiences in life led to their being uncomfortable with conflict; what strategies they had learned early on in their arguing history that kept them from discussing problems civilly now. I also found that certain temperaments and personalities find arguments to be inconsistent with how they see themselves. I realized I had to ask myself for each couple, "What do they do when they have a disagreement?"

The focus of my treatment became less on general conflict management strategies or improving communication skills.

Instead, I have learned to focus first on what was causing resentments in the marriage and then how to help my clients find strategies that make their arguments more bearable, more tolerable, more respectful, and more productive. Learning how to stay in the ring until the issue is resolved is a key turning point. The reason this is key is that when the discomfort can be tolerated, issues can be resolved. When issues can be resolved, the couple develops hope. When the couple has hope about their future, they can let go of some of the resentments of the past.

So where does resentment and resentment dynamics come in? Remember how we discussed what happens when couples have years of arguments without closure? Resentment is the fruit of years of unresolved issues. The problem is that if you can't get closure, if you can't resolve your issues, if you can't stay in the ring and get closure on the issue enough to resolve it, *where does the problem go*?

In a healthy relationship if a couple has an issue regarding money, parenting, sex, chores, spending, etc., the majority of couples find a way to discuss the problem. There are detours, some interrupting, and a degree of discomfort (especially for the member that bears the most responsibility for the argument). However, after some awkwardness and emotional pain, the couple finds a way to ask, "So what is the plan?", or, "How are we going to compromise?" These couples manage their emotions better than most. They stay more respectful. There is less interrupting and harsh words. These couples have fewer detours to dead end arguments or needless guilt inductions and, generally, the volume of the discussion stays lower. As a couple, they stay in the ring and eventually resolve the problem. It is as if the problem goes away.

But what if they can't resolve their problem? What if there is too much focus on bringing up things from the past? Or name calling? Or rolling the eyes? What if there is bullying or intimidation? What if the couple goes down every path other than the one that leads to resolving the issue? These are the couples that can't resolve their issues. These are the ones who can't discuss the problem and reach an agreement they can both live with and ultimately stick to. What happens to the issue if you can't resolve it?

What these couples do is this: *They open up the basement door, and they kick the issue down in the basement, and slam the basement door. Then at some point they 'make up.'* They act as if the issue has gone away, but it doesn't go away. If they have the ability to get in the ring and resolve the issue at hand, it does go away. However, if they can't resolve it and they kick it down in the basement, it goes down in the basement with 10 years (or however old the relationship is) of other gunk and junk and unresolved issues. It gets all funky and smelly. That smell is RESENTMENT. As the resentment starts to build up in a relationship, it starts to permeate the relationship and all they smell when they come home (because it works its way through the floorboards), is anger, bitterness, and dislike for their partner. When this happens, they start to drift away from their partner emotionally. When couples realize that they do not have the ability to resolve their differences, something happens to their relationship. *They lose hope.*

When couples lose hope that they can constructively work out their problems, there are changes in the way that the couple interacts with each other. My experience is that little issues act as triggers (thus generating a resentment dynamic) and are magnified when there is no chance of dealing with any of the problems. After time, all couples ask themselves, "Can we resolve our differences or not?"

In dynamics where the couples do not have the tools to resolve their differences, resentment builds up. The couple loses hope that they will ever be able to rebuild the love and connection that characterized the early part of the relationship. There are not enough extended periods of calm when emotional healing can occur; long periods of time when the couple just gets along well. When this happens, the couple starts to grow apart and small changes start to creep into the way that they interact with each other. These changes affect the level of connectedness and the couple's ability to open up to each other. In other words it affects their level of intimacy.

Chapter Two

WHAT IS
A RESENTMENT
DYNAMIC?

When feelings get hurt, a resentment dynamic may be formed. A resentment dynamic is a series of events that are fueled by a couple's response to a problem; usually a behavior by one or both of the individuals in the relationship. This behavior causes feelings to be hurt and people to be discouraged and frustrated. In a true dynamic there is a downward spiral in the couple's level of satisfaction, happiness, and connectedness. This downward spiral is due to the behaviors that follow the initial trigger event.

In a typical resentment dynamic, these behaviors lead to feelings of resentment and small changes in the way that we feel about our mates. These in turn lead to changes in the way we think about them. This in turn leads to small changes in the way that we treat them around the house. We start to do things that are in our best interest, not our mate's. This may be short-lived or more long lasting. If the changes are long lasting, they create a new way that we treat them. This may include treating them with contempt, disrespect, or being more distant.

When we change the way we treat our mates, this usually leads to a change in the way that they feel about us. As would be expected, this in turn usually leads to a change in the way that they treat and respond to us in return. There is a sense that things are different. Sometimes there is an understanding about what is generating this change in relations, but men in particular are often unclear as to the source of the problem until it is almost too late. In a typical resentment dynamic, there is a downward spiral of behaviors and responses to these behaviors that causes a cascade of problems within the relationship. The reality is that there are things we will do for our mates when we are getting along with them that we won't do for them when we are angry or feel emotionally disconnected.

It is not uncommon in the process of developing a resentment dynamic that one or both individuals in the relationship will start to put more energy into some other activity such as drinking or drug use, shopping or their career.

If there is an effort to identify the trouble early on in the cycle, there is a good chance that long lasting problems within the relationship can be avoided. However, if there is any tendency to ignore the problem (men tend to do this but by no means have a monopoly on the strategy), it may cause greater problems, and, eventually, anger and alienation forms. Catching a resentment dynamic early is essential in minimizing the effects on a relationship. Resentment dynamics are a negative feedback loop. This means that they fuel themselves. Do you have a resentment dynamic or a "downward spiral" in your relationship? How do you get off the train and snip this dynamic?

An example might be a husband who works hard at his job. He focuses much of his waking time on his job; spending 50 or 60 hours a week at his workplace. This may cause a dynamic where the wife feels that she is second or third on his list of priorities and starts to harbor resentment about the lack of assistance she is getting with parenting, not as much help around the house, etc. Due to this resentment, she may start to focus on how the children are suffering from lack of parental nurturance. This may lead to her hyper-focusing on the children to make up for the lack of parenting time. Ultimately, the husband feels that he is second on his wife's list of priorities and this fuels his resentment and alienation. After a period of time and with growing levels of alienation, the couple's level of intimacy deteriorates, as does the frequency of sexual involvement. This leads to growing marital dissatisfaction for both the husband and wife. The husband starts to really spend time at the office because it is the only place he feels successful and comfortable. The wife focuses less and less on the husband. She does not feel as emotionally connected to him as she has in the past. After all, he is distant and hardly ever there. She concentrates her energies on her children and home; thus validates to the husband that she does not care for him, that he is not her priority, that she got what she wanted from the marriage (children), and that he has no hope this relationship will ever be the one he dreamed about. He becomes sexually frustrated and easily agitated due to feeling that his home life is out of control and that his needs are not being met. Naturally, he becomes vulnerable to seduction by another female or he may simply continue to distance himself. As he distances himself more and more, this does not make the wife feel emotionally connected to him. In fact, she feels disconnected and not at all understood.

Most women report that when they feel emotionally disconnected, they start to feel uncomfortable in sharing their feelings or their bodies. As the cycle continues there is a series of accusations and growing frustration which is fueled by the inability to get at the heart of the problem. It is not uncommon at this point to have each member of the couple try to hurt the other in some way. This is either out of frustration or to vent their anger at what they see as the other having caused them so much pain and discouragement.

As I noted earlier, there are things that we will do for our mates when we are getting along with them that we will not do when we feel emotionally disconnected. The kissing, back rubs, touching, and words of support (coming up behind our mates and saying, "Don't worry we will get through this") all dry up.

Resentment dynamics are usually generated or started by a trigger event. Usually these are behaviors that are implicitly understood as something that is going to cause a problem if one or both members of the pair choose to engage in it. Sometimes it is not the behavior itself, but how often it is engaged in. Either way, triggers are understood by a couple as something that will cause a problem.

Some triggers are not behaviors that have historically caused problems. However, they can still serve to generate resentment. Examples of a trigger event might include spending too much money, physical abuse, or substance abuse. Some behaviors are acceptable as long as they don't occur too often. For example, there is an agreed upon limit or number of times that one may engage in this behavior. If one of you makes a choice to go over the limit, there are going to be repercussions. Examples that I frequently see are spending too much time at work, spending too much money shopping, or spending too much time on hobbies (such as hunting too often or golfing too much).

All relationships have resentment dynamics. Good relationships have only one or two mild ones. Dysfunctional relationships have several severe dynamics. My experience is that it only takes one resentment dynamic, if it is significant enough, to end a relationship.

Though some couples may be able to identify a full resentment dynamic, there are usually several dynamics at play within any given relationship. Some resentment dynamics are easy to identify once a couple understands what they need to look for. Therapy may be needed to uncover some of the more subtle dynamics. It is important to identify and resolve both the major and minor problem cycles within a relationship in order for healing to occur. Once major problems have been resolved, the relationship can be so damaged by the arguing and hurt that eventually minor problems are magnified. These minor problems still have the potential to undo the healing that has occurred. For this reason, it may make sense to seek the help of a third party that can help identify these and assist in the developing of strategies for breaking these cycles.

Much of what a couple needs to learn to improve their marriage can be learned from reading books on the subject. However, some problems such as understanding their resentment dynamic may require a couple to seek professional help. Some insightful couples may be able to identify the dynamic that repeatedly causes them problems and leads to the greatest levels of resentment, but many cannot.

The concept of a resentment dynamic suggests that every relationship, no matter how new or old it is, no matter how satisfying or unhappy it is, has a series of dynamics. These dynamics imply that there is a behavior that one of the parties engages in which bothers or angers the other. This could be golfing with their friends too much or spending too much money when they go shopping.

Now, sometimes bothers is too mild a word and in some instances our mates really make us angry when they engage in certain behaviors. When we realize what they have done, and depending on how angry it makes us and how many times they have done it, we react to their behavior with a response of our own. Our behavior, or how we react to the thing that they did, changes the nature of the relationship.

The reality is we are now upset with one of the very people that we care most about in the whole world. This is difficult and makes most of us very uncomfortable. We don't like to be upset with the people that we love. It also causes us to ask ourselves a number of questions: "Why are they doing this? Are they not aware that it bothers me? Did they think that I was stupid, and I wouldn't notice? Do they have a problem with the behavior? Is it a compulsion that they have a hard time controlling and they just don't see? Do they care more for the feeling they get when they engage in the behavior than they do for me? Surely they must or they would not have done it, right? We agreed after the last time that they would stop doing this so why can't they keep their part of the bargain? Are they liars? Have I married someone who is going to just do whatever they want, whenever they want in the relationship and I just have to stand here and take it? Am I married to someone I can't trust?"

All kinds of things go through our minds when this happens. When we start asking ourselves these kinds of questions, it is natural for this to affect our moods and our sense of comfort when we are around our mates. We tend to be colder to them; we tend to be more distant with them. Part of us wants to punish them for their behavior and how it has affected the relationship. Part of us just naturally withdraws from them. We give them the cold shoulder. This affects the vibe or comfort level of the relationship. As would be expected, this change in the comfort or intimacy level of the relationship is sensed by our partner and they respond, usually, in a less than positive way. This changes the tone or level of comfort within the relationship.

Naturally, we respond to this change in the comfort level that has generally characterized the relationship. *This reacting to each other's behavior, the resentment it brings, the change in level of happiness/comfort, and the eventual emotional withdrawal creates a negative downward spiral in the relationship.* A negative downward spiral means that much like a strand of DNA or water in a toilet that has been flushed, it swirls and swirls ever downward until it is gone. Our relationships can go down the drain as well, unless we understand our resentment dynamics, actively address the behaviors that are fueling them, and address the way that we respond.

The issue is not whether there is a dynamic produced, but rather how severe a dynamic is generated. Is it significant enough to produce long-term negative effects? How long have these resentment dynamics persisted? How forgiving are you as a person?

The issue of how many dynamics is pertinent because it asks the question, "How many of the dynamics are fueled by my behavior and how many are fueled by my partner's? Am I willing to forgive some of their behaviors if they forgive some of mine?" In most relationships, some of the resentments are resolved and some are not. Most couples hold out hope that they have the tools in their collective tool box to ultimately resolve their problem. Most of the couples that seek my services do not.

Healthy Couples

What I see in healthy, well-adjusted couples is this: these couples have issues, as all couples do. These include issues like spending differences, disagreements over parenting, arguments over how often they want sex, hobbies, and interests (such as friends or golfing). Frequently, there are issues related to disagreements over how much each is expected to do in terms of chores or spending too much time at work.

Whatever the problem is, most couples seem to be able to get in the ring and resolve their problem. Yes, they may get angry or frustrated. Chances are good, however, that they are civil and respectful when they have a disagreement. They probably sat down when they spoke to each other vs. standing and getting in each other's faces. They probably spoke to each other in respectful tones and did not interrupt or roll their eyes at each other. After listening to each other's point of view, they decided how much of the issue they agreed on or how far apart they were. Then, either one or both of them compromised, relented, and gave in because it was important to them. Sometimes they agreed to disagree on the issue all together (you can do this on a limited basis as long as it is not the predominant strategy). In the end, they made an agreement they ultimately kept or stuck to; communicating trust in their word.

What generates a resentment dynamic, and thus causes the greatest problems, is **when a couple lacks the ability to get in the ring to resolve difficult issues**. Usually this involves couples that yell at each other, interrupt, or roll their eyes. I absolutely guarantee that an issue won't be resolved if a couple points their fingers at each other or starts swearing. I use the metaphor of getting in the ring a lot in this book because it is a very important skill that a couple either has or doesn't have (and if they do not have it, they need to learn it).

So why is it so difficult to get in the ring? Ultimately, if we have difficulty getting "in the ring" or if we are reluctant to get "in the ring," it may be because we fear the emotions that are released when we do. Maybe we fear talking about the problem because it makes us feel uncomfortable. Maybe it taps into the feelings we had when we were children; pulled into the principal's office or having to be talked to by our parents. Perhaps we fear overreacting and letting our anger out.

What I have found is that we fear being rejected by the person we love the most. It is difficult to tolerate having the person we love being upset with us. The great irony here is that, in facing our fears and staying in the ring, we keep our love, but in giving in to our fears of being rejected (and fleeing), we end up losing our connection. If we want our partner to be able to tolerate getting in the ring or staying in the ring until there is resolution to a problem, we often need to be able to convince them that we are "not going to leave."

Sitting across from a couple and watching them argue tells me a lot about how they argue in private. Initially, they start out civilly. In the end though, they revert to old time- honored strategies (trying to hurt the other with words, bringing up issues from the past, going down every path but the one leading to resolution or simply saying, "OK, you are right" to get out of the ring because it is becoming too intense or they are fearful of the other). Eventually, they reveal themselves and how they actually argue in private.

Chapter Three

HOW RESENTMENT AFFECTS INTIMACY

What does it mean to be intimate? The term 'intimacy' comes from the Latin word 'intima,' meaning innermost or core. At our cores are the things we are worried about— the things that we are thinking about. Our intimaes also hold those things about us that we fear are broken or less than perfect. Our intima holds those childlike emotions that we share with our lovers or our children. Intimacy is the willingness and the ability to self-disclose those most sacred of inner thoughts and feelings. It is what is going on in our head. Our ability to be REAL is what is in our intima.

The expression "being intimate" means being open and honest with people. Our intimates are those with whom we can let down our guard. Everybody that we meet gets some access to our intima. The metaphor I use is like a shirt with three buttons. How many buttons do you unbutton? For the majority of people we meet, we unbutton ourselves one button. We show them only a small portion of our inner world. We share information about ourselves or show them some of the things that we have been thinking about. To our friends and those that we trust, we are able to reveal even more about ourselves. We unbutton ourselves two buttons for these people. We share with them our fears or the things that we are worried about. The nature of sharing intimate things is that we are communicating, "I trust you with the information that I am sharing. I know that you will honor it and not use it to hurt me or share it with others." We must trust them in order to reveal our innermost thoughts and fears because we lay ourselves bare before anyone that we share this level of disclosure with.

The third button, or opening oneself up intimately, is the ability to truly share our feelings, thoughts, and concerns in an atmosphere of total acceptance. It is in this atmosphere that we match the level of disclosure that our partners or friends engage in and vice versa. Each person has an inner circle of people that they are truly intimate with. This means people who know their flaws; those secret parts of them which are broken or less than perfect and these people accept them despite their flaws. These are the people who are privy to the third button or access to our cores. With them, we are able to be entirely honest and hold little information back. We share our dreams and those deepest feelings that define us.

I laughingly say sometimes that there is a fourth button but behind that lays our sexual fantasies and private dreams. The point I am trying to make is that we have levels of vulnerability that we are willing to tolerate. The main criteria is that we have to be willing to trust the individual we are being intimate with in order to open up emotionally with them.

But let me be plain: intimacy is a HUGE issue, especially for women (and about half of all men). If your mate has said, "I don't' feel emotionally connected to you anymore," what they are probably saying is, "I don't feel that you open up and share your inner world with me anymore or I don't feel that I want to open up and share with you." Take note, these are very important messages and should not be ignored.

When Resentment Builds

What happens when issues are not being resolved or when people do not stay in the ring long enough to get closure on important issues? What happens when over time, people lose hope of ever being able to resolve their issues with their mates and resentments build? What happens is that the laughing, teasing, joking, and interest in sex start to dry up and we start to grow apart. In essence, we go from having access to our partner's inner world to getting almost nothing. We go from having access to their third button ... to no buttons at all. They no longer trust us enough to allow us into their inner world. This promotes a growing apart. When this happens, couples start to not allow the partner, who used to have an all-access pass, into their world. We don't want to share with them or simply can't share with them. It makes us too anxious. We don't know if we can trust them. The frustrated partner usually senses this and starts to ask questions to test how much access they have, asking, "What are you thinking?" We must then ask ourselves, do we let our guard down or not? Do we lower our fences and let them in, or do we say, "Oh, nothing," or "I don't know."

When couples reach this level of disconnectedness, ultimately, they report feeling like they are roommates and not husband and wife. When we sense that we are no longer given access to our mate's inner world, we sometimes overreact and attempt to pry out the information we want from them. This means that we ask pointed questions or put pressure on our mates to open up. The natural outcome of this, however, is opening up even less access, not more.

Why is it that many couples live happily for five, ten, twelve years before they start to have problems? In many cases, there tends to be a critical mass of resentment built-up before it starts to affect the intimacy level of the relationship. At the end of the day, however, we feel like we are living like "Roommates".

Chapter Four

Beth and Carl

Beth and Carl came to my practice seeking help with their marriage. Beth was a successful real estate agent while Carl was an English teacher at a local high school. Married for thirteen years, most of those years had been fairly satisfying. They had dated for almost two years prior to marrying and felt that they knew each other quite well prior to becoming engaged. Beth stated early on in the therapy process that she felt that Carl was her best friend for most of the relationship. This was one of the reasons why their problems were so disturbing for her. She reported that she felt not only was she losing her marriage, but that she had already lost her best friend. Carl echoed these sentiments and stated that he very much missed the feelings that he had felt toward Beth earlier in their relationship. Both agreed, the first few years of their marriage were quite satisfying.

Both agreed that with the birth of their first child, things changed in the relationship. Carl indicated that Beth had a difficult pregnancy and experienced minor symptoms of postpartum depression after the birth of their first daughter. He tearfully stated that Beth was moody, cried often, and seemed unhappy after the baby's birth. This surprised him, since he and Beth had been very excited about the prospect of becoming parents. Carl reported that with Beth's depression came moodiness and irritability that he had not seen prior to this. He stated that one of the things that he found so attractive about Beth was her up-beat nature and how she rarely let little things get to her.

Beth agreed that this was not a good time in her life. She stated that she was confused at her depression and did not understand why she was so depressed about something that she wanted so badly. Beth herself admitted that she was easily frustrated, cried for no reason, had no sex drive, and wondered for several months if she was even capable of bonding with her baby. Carl reported that for several months after the baby's birth there was no sexual activity at all in their relationship. While this was difficult, it was in no way a deal breaker for their relationship. Beth stated that after struggling with her feelings for three months, she finally talked to her OB/GYN and was placed on an antidepressant medication. She stated that this helped dramatically and that she felt like her old self within a month. While her feelings of depression were improved by the addition of an anti-depressant, Beth felt both more tired at the end of the day and less interested in sex with her husband.

Beth stated that Carl was a good father; routinely getting up in the middle of the night to feed their daughter and helping with more chores around the house than he had prior to the pregnancy. As Beth came out of her depression, she started to feel more connected to her baby and eventually felt the kind of happiness and connection to her baby that she had been dreaming about.

Things in the relationship seemed to be getting better; so much better, in fact, that the couple decided to try and have another child. This attempt was successful and after an uneventful pregnancy, Beth gave birth to another baby girl. With another child came the satisfaction that Beth had been wanting in her life and she stated that she was happier than she had been in years. Carl, on the other hand, was less satisfied and reported that he felt that he was now, "third or fourth on Beth's list of priorities," behind their children, the house, and Beth's career. Carl complained that Beth was so tired after working and caring for the children that she rarely felt like making love. He stated, "Sex isn't everything, but it was one of the things that made me so attracted to Beth." Carl felt resentful that he was not a priority in Beth's life and that his needs were not more important. He felt that he was doing what she asked around the house in terms of the care of their children but was not getting what he wanted, which was more time alone with Beth and more physical intimacy.

When asked what kept Carl and Beth from having more time alone, she stated that after working forty hours a week and commuting for almost eight hours a week, she felt that she was away from her children too much as it was. She felt guilty about getting a babysitter and going out with Carl on weekend nights. Because of this, she made excuses or simply said, "No, I won't enjoy it", when Carl made statements about going out to dinner.

Carl communicated that he felt neglected by Beth and resented the fact that she was putting her energy into the care of the children and her career. He admitted that arguments started to become more common and more intense when they did have them. He and Beth started to argue about things that had not been issues before. Now they were arguing about money and how each was spending it. They also argued about when they would go to Beth's parent's house, which was on the East Coast. According to Carl, they also frequently argued about his work schedule and how much time he was spending at work. They both stated that their arguments were (more often than not) simply a legitimized opportunity to vent one's frustration and anger on the other. Their words were hurtful and hard, rather than soft and conciliatory. They admitted that swearing and name-calling had become more frequent.

When asked if they ever resolved their differences, they both looked at each other and admitted that they knew what the other was angry about, but never felt that they got closure to their arguments or issues. Carl felt that Beth took their arguing sessions as an opportunity to bring up issues from the past or to vent her frustration at him for other things that he was doing, rather than focus on the one problem that they were really arguing about. This meant that the disagreement had no focus. Beth stated that resolving disputes with Carl became more and more difficult since he would become angry and scream and swear. His size and presence, coupled with his anger, often scared her and she admitted that she would eventually back down and simply say, "Whatever", rather than continue the disagreement until they had resolution.

These two individuals presented an almost classic example of a resentment dynamic. The relationship started out with very few problems and was initially an example of two well-adjusted individuals who were well-matched and who really cared for each other. With the addition of children, however, there was, for Beth, an increase in fatigue and the prioritizing of children in the relationship. This caused resentment on the part of Carl and he changed the way he interacted with Beth. Carl admitted that as his sexual frustration increased, he became more and more resentful toward Beth and started to spend more and more time at work or with friends. He admitted that he stopped listening to Beth when she talked about things at work or with the children. These were sensitive subjects and often made him angry as opposed to connected with Beth and her life. Carl's working more and being away from the family, as well as his focus on his friends and seeming indifference to their shared life, gave Beth more ammunition for arguments and justified her feeling that Carl cared more for his job and friends than he did for her and the children. With these increased feelings of being emotionally disconnected from Carl and resentful herself, Beth started to feel less and less sexual toward Carl.

With these changes came a distance between Carl and Beth that had not been there previously. The term that both used to describe the relationship was awkward. Gone were the comfortable days prior to the children; when they had talked for hours about their dreams and what was going on in each other's lives. Now, they rarely asked about each other's lives. When they did talk, their communication was characterized by lack of eye contact, brief statements meant to communicate basic information having to do with the children, or management of the home. These words had a thin veneer of civility on them, but were covering a deep pool of frustration and resentment. Their sex life had gone from being something that was frequent and satisfying (a way that both used to stay emotionally connected), to infrequent and unsatisfying. Carl stated that even when they did make love, it lacked the passion that it had in the past and felt that Beth was only, "throwing me some crumbs to keep me and my resources in the relationship." Beth herself admitted that she didn't really feel as emotionally connected to Carl as she had been in the past and that since she needed that sense of intimacy to feel sexual, it was difficult to make love. She stated that sex for her was an intensely emotional act. She stated that she had difficulty relaxing during sex since looking at Carl and having him on top of her was difficult and awkward. She agreed with Carl that it felt fake and contrived, not sincere, as it had been in the past. Beth stated that she also felt that she was being duplicitous or fake and that she was sending Carl false messages about where they were in the relationship.

This is where Carl and Beth entered into treatment with me. They were referred by former clients of mine that worked with Beth. Beth was interested in improving her communication with Carl. Carl was less hopeful about the relationship improving and seemed reluctant to believe that things could be better between him and Beth. After listening to both of their accounts about what happened in the relationship and noting that there was little actual disagreement, I discussed with them how my approach was different from other therapists. They both agreed that I was not the first marriage counselor that they had seen. (They had visited with another therapist a year-and-a-half prior to meeting with me.) Both agreed that the two sessions they had completed with that therapist were helpful. However, they did not feel that improving their communication skills was going to resolve their differences or help them feel emotionally closer to each other. For this reason, they had not returned to that therapist and continued on the path they had started.

Beth reported that since they had ended therapy with the prior counselor, she had occasionally read self-help books about how they spoke different languages and how they needed to appreciate how each of them showed they cared for each other. These also were helpful but did not ultimately bring them together emotionally. It seemed that too much damage had been done and that it was going to take a drastic change in the way that each of them interacted in order to avoid a divorce.

After listening to their story, I discussed how I approached couples counseling differently than most therapists. I shared with them the metaphor of what do we do with issues if they go unresolved and how these inevitably end up in the basement. They shared how their friends had talked about their own basement and how this seemed to resonate with their problems as well. Beth and Carl left the first session with some hope that they could improve their relationship and avoid the divorce that neither wanted.

After discussing the metaphor of the basement, I went on to go over the blame game with Carl and Beth. The blame game, as the name suggests, implies that most couples spend a good deal of time blaming each other for the couple's problems and taking little or no responsibility for one's own role in the deteriorating relationship. We also went over how this strategy doesn't work. What I tell clients is that the normal strategy is to point fingers at each other and expect the other person to change. I explained to them that the responsibility for how the problem got the way it did is shared between both of them. If we partition out the responsibility for how the couple got the way it is, do they know what their portion of the problem is? In other words, what do they do that causes problems in the relationship?

Most people know that their behavior causes problems, but they are usually only aware of how the big things they do cause problems. Do they truly know where all of their partner's resentment is coming from? Don't they need to? I have my clients complete a questionnaire I call the **Resentment Rating Scale**. By completing the Resentment Rating Scale, they get a better idea of all of the things, major and minor, that they do to each other which causes problems.

At this point, I place a pen on the 8x10 rug of my office and ask Carl, "If we partition this out, what portion of the burden for how the situation got the way it did belongs to you?" I show him the two edges of my rug. One end would be taking 100 percent of the responsibility. On the other end would be taking 0 percent of the fault. Carl, as many people do, placed the pen in the middle. He stated, "Right there, about half." Now, I am always a little leery of this. What are the chances that he has half and she has half? It seems a little too safe. When I confronted him on this, he stated, "Well maybe not quite that much." He moved the pen to represent this. When I asked, "What do you do that causes this amount of problems?" His response was not uncommon: "I know most of the things, I work a lot and I have been hanging out with my friends more." Carl was aware of most of the bigger things that he was doing, but was unaware of all of the things that Beth was angry about.

Next, I asked Beth what she felt her amount of responsibility was. I prompted her to not feel like she needed to take what was left on my rug, but to put the pen where she felt it really belonged; to only take that portion of the responsibility she felt she truly deserved. Beth placed the pen at about the half-way point. When I asked what she felt her portion of the responsibility was for problems in the relationship, she was quick to answer. Beth admitted that she focused a good deal of her time on the children. She stated that she had always dreamed of having children and that she was happiest when she was playing with her girls. She also stated that focusing on the children had started to take up more and more of her time since her relationship with her husband had started to deteriorate.

Our second session started out by having both Carl and Beth complete my Resentment Rating Scale. Having done this hundreds of times with previous clients, I was not surprised to find that both harbored a great deal of resentment toward each other. I normally concentrate, at least initially, on those items that are marked as either a '4' or '5' on the rating scale. In this case, much of Beth's resentment was due to what she perceived as Carl's being overly focused on working, spending time with friends, and feeling pressure to have sex. She also scored as a five the statement Lack of Intimacy, i.e., no interest in talking, "I don't feel emotionally connected to you."

Carl's rating scale showed issues related to Beth putting too much energy into the children and the house. He was also sexually frustrated and felt that they as a couple did not resolve their differences. He essentially did not feel that he was a priority since Beth now had the children that she had always wanted.

As I normally do, at the end of this session, I asked each to rate their level of connectedness. I ask them to pick a number between 1 and 10 that most accurately represents how they feel toward their partner. In this continuum '10' means extremely connected, and like a soul mate. The number '5' represents a feeling of "do I stay or do I go," meaning that if you asked me any time today I might give you a different answer. Either, "yes, I am going to stay" or "no, I am ready to leave." A '1' means that I am absolutely indifferent to you and your pain; I don't care about you at all and hope that you find someone else, that I am done with you emotionally.

Now, this can be an eye opening (and sometimes hurtful) period of the session. I asked Beth the question first. What would she rate her current feelings for Carl? What she stated came as no surprise to me, but I believe Carl was somewhat taken back. Beth reported that she was a '5', that she did not feel connected to Carl emotionally and that there were times she wanted to work on things. There were times that she wanted to simply get a divorce and move on with her life. The look on

Carl's face was dramatic. His mouth dropped open and he had a look of astonishment. His eyes did not hide his hurt feelings.

As I normally do, I ask the second part of the question: "If you are a 5, what would Carl have to do to make this a 5.5?" She stated that she would feel more connected to Carl if he would come home at 5:00 and not work on Saturdays. I asked Carl if this was something that he could do as a means of showing he was invested in the process of trying to improve things with Beth. He agreed and stated that he would work less and come home earlier.

I asked Carl the same question: What number he would be on a scale of 1-10? Carl somewhat surprised me when he said he was a '7'. I was prepared for a number much closer to Beth's. This was good news because it also gave me important information; it suggested that Beth was the one who was the least happy person in the relationship. Now that I knew this, focusing on keeping Beth in the relationship was one of my key agendas.

When I asked Carl what would make him a '7.5', he stated, "Feeling that I was a higher priority in Beth's life." For him, this meant being acknowledged when he came home from work and carving time out for them to have a date night. Carl wanted to be able to have time to focus on just him and Beth. Beth felt guilty about taking time for her and Carl since she had to spend so much time away from their children to begin with. Beth quickly agreed to this and the couple's homework was to pick an evening on the weekend, to get a babysitter, and go out for dinner.

On our next session I had Beth and Carl complete the **Barriers to Resolving Conflict Questionnaire**. When Beth and Carl completed the Barriers To Resolving Conflict Questionnaire, they both acknowledged that bringing up issues from the past and extreme intensity were issues for both of them. Beth stated that for her, Carl's seeming to be more interested in trying to hurt her with words than resolving the problem and swearing came up as issues. Carl placed, stopping because Beth started to cry as one of the main reasons that they did not discuss issues until they were resolved.

I normally spend quite a bit of time going through the barriers that couples report as reasons that they don't resolve their issues. In this case, Beth admitted that she would cry when arguments became too heated. She did not do this as a manipulation or to make Carl stop; it was just a natural response when she became emotional. Carl was frustrated because he would start to feel guilty and would become uncomfortable when Beth started to cry. This would shut him down and keep him from continuing with the discussion.

Bringing up issues from the past were both problems that Carl and Beth agreed were causing them to get out of the ring. Carl admitted that when he lost his temper he would swear or call Beth names. Beth stated that when Carl became too angry, she started to shutdown. This was not because Carl had ever hurt her physically. These conditions tapped into Beth's past and she admitted that she frequently just stopped the disagreement by stating, "OK, OK," or by saying, "whatever." Beth admitted that she had been raised in a home with a rage-aholic father. He would frequently berate Beth and yell and scream when he was upset. This had always troubled Beth and she admitted that she was sensitive to feelings getting too uncomfortable or the disagreement becoming too loud. She realized that this did not help to solve the problems, but she felt helpless to stop her own discomfort.

Bringing up problems from the past was meant to show their partner that there was a long history of making decisions that harmed the relationship. However, in reality, bringing up issues from the past actually shuts down the discussion. They agreed to help each other to focus more on the issues they were arguing about and less on making a case about the other's poor choices.

One of the things that is powerful about understanding the role of the barriers is that when armed with this insight, a couple can now be aware of when this is happening in a discussion and power through their temptation to use or succumb to them. This can be *difficult* or *really difficult*. I warned them that just because they knew what they needed to do differently didn't mean it would magically change the way they argue. What I find more often than not is that once a couple has bought into my philosophy, they have renewed hope about their relationship and make new efforts to change the way they argue.

The first thing I try to accomplish at this point is to assist the couple to have a discussion, but to experience a different outcome; a different result than the usual outcome which would normally be to start to discuss an issue and have the discussion turn into an argument. The argument gets intense and then the couple starts to use their tried and true strategies to resolve it. They stop the resolution process due to the aforementioned problems. Often the outcome is very different when they try to have a discussion, they are *aware of their tendencies,* and are in the safety of my office.

Normally, I start with a safe issue which is minor and that can be easily resolved: thus giving the couple hope that they can do this on their own. This was not what happened in the case of Carl and Beth.

When asked what problem they would like to try and resolve, they both agreed they would like to solve a problem that had plagued Carl and Beth for years. The issue was, "When do we go to Beth's parent's house in Rhode Island?" Historically, this issue had brought up a lot of anger and resentment. Carl's parents lived nearby and he had a moderately connected relationship with them. He stated that he would call his parents once every two weeks and visit them once a month. Beth, however, was much closer with her parents and wanted to maintain that degree of connectedness she had traditionally had. She also wanted her children to have a good relationship with their grandparents and she wanted them to bond.

The realities of limited vacation time left for some hurt feelings. Carl liked to take the children for a vacation in the summer and to use some vacation time throughout the year as well. He was OK with the idea of getting away to Beth's family for one week a year, but no more than that. Beth was resentful about this and, if given the choice, would have used most, if not all, of her vacation time to take her and the kids to her parent's house. Surprising to me was the fact that this issue had not been discussed prior to Beth and Carl getting married. So, they needed to find a win/win that was acceptable for both of them.

This issue was causing a great deal of underlying bitterness between the two of them; so for them, it became the natural choice of decisions to try and resolve in my office. We started out by trying to determine where each of them was in terms of "what would you like the picture to look like." Beth stated that she would like to fly the entire family to Rhode Island for at least two weeks a year. She wanted to spend Christmas through New Year's every year as well as a week in the summer. She wanted to spend the rest of her vacation every other year on a vacation with just Carl and then every other year to split it up and take the kids on some long weekends.

Carl, as stated earlier, is a teacher, he does not get a lot of time off during the school year, but gets the summer, Christmas break, and spring break off. He reiterated how difficult and stressful his job was and how he needed breaks to relax and unwind. Carl liked Beth's family, but felt that a whole week was a long time to spend with them. They were nurturing and kind people, and he knew that Beth enjoyed being with them. However, he admitted that he felt out of place and after a day or two became bored and wished he were home. Carl stated that he would prefer to alternate; spending every other Thanksgiving break with them and then every other Christmas for three or four days. He also stated that he was OK with the idea of Beth taking the kids to her parent's for a week in the summer as well–as long as she was alright with the idea of him not going along.

Neither was surprised to hear the other's point of view. Nevertheless, in the past they had been unable to find a compromise that they could both agree to. As they became more alienated from each other, they had even less success. Armed with their newfound resolve to settle this problem and in the safety of my office, we proceeded. Beth went first.

I stopped Beth and Carl at this point in the discussion to bring attention to what had happened. The discussion had started out in the right direction, but as they both reached for issues from the past that both were angry about, the focus quickly changed from problem resolution to trying to hurt each other with words. They agreed that though they had tried to stay on topic, as their partner pushed their buttons, things quickly deteriorated. I asked, "Is this what your arguments look like at home?" They both agreed.

Armed with this insight, they made a second attempt to resolve the issue of when to visit Beth's parents. With this recent failure in the front of their minds, the second attempt to reach a compromise was much more successful. Carl started first and offered to go to Christmas with Beth's parents if they only stayed for six days. He also stated that he did not care how long she and the kids went over the summer as long as they didn't mind that he did not go with them. Beth was surprised to hear this and stated that she was actually pretty OK with this compromise. She did want one additional thing: it was important for her to send a positive message to her parents. She went on to state that she would appreciate it if he would go to her parents for the 4th of July weekend or drive them there and then fly back. Carl agreed to this compromise and they ceremoniously shook hands. Beth was guardedly optimistic and stated that she was happy that Carl was willing to go with her over Christmas, but admitted that she was concerned that he would become bored and make her visit miserable since he really didn't want to go. Carl admitted that he was not crazy about the idea but wanted to improve things with Beth, so he was willing to "start first." He did want Beth to appreciate his concession and forgive him if he went for a walk without the kids or if he went to the library in Providence. She agreed. In fact, she smiled for the first time since I had met her.

Two weeks later with some basic information about what was causing their sense of connectedness to be lost and what tools they needed in their collective toolboxes to deal with these issues, we changed our focus. The focus at this point in therapy was now on, "What is different in your relationship." They agreed that there had been an increase in their sense of hope since they had come to an agreement on the largest of their issues; when to go to Rhode Island. Beth stated that they had been carving out time for a date night and that this had ended in her and Carl making love for the first time in over three months. Carl was happy with this and noticed a general warming from Beth in terms of how she talked to him.

This is the point in therapy where the focus changes from the issues causing resentment to the opposite of a resentment dynamic, which is an intimacy dynamic. An intimacy dynamic is where a couple starts to do nice things for each other in an attempt to see how good they can get it. In this case, there was both a carving out of time for each other as well as a sense that each was looking at each other more and being more respectful when they did talk to each other. Carl stated that Beth was once again willing to talk about his work stresses and he, in turn, was coming home earlier.

At the end of this session, we discussed where both Carl and Beth were on my scale of 1-10. I asked Carl first. He looked at Beth and stated, "I am probably a '7.5' or an '8.'" When I asked him what it would take for him to be a solid '8', he stated, "Really just more of the same." This is a common response. Once they have the intimacy dynamic started, most things start to improve on their own. Things start to thaw between them, so they start to put more energy into this. Once things have improved a bit, there is a lingering sense of let's see how long it lasts now. This means that before they really open their hearts up that last bit (because they can get hurt), they want to be sure these changes are integrated. They want to be sure that the changes are real and now part of how they do business.

This is not surprising since many couples admit that there have been points in the past where their partner wanted something so they were able to be nice to them for two or three weeks. Once this concern is resolved, however, the couple is allowed to go to even deeper levels of connectedness and trust because they realize that the changes that are being made are real and will probably be sustained.

When Beth and Carl returned two weeks later, there was a noticeable difference in the way they looked at each other. They sat closer to each other on the couch and Beth had her hand on Carl's leg much of the session. Gone was the lack of eye contact and the anger in their voices. They looked at each other when they talked, they did not interrupt each other, and they laughed at each other several times during the hour. They reported they had finally been able to resolve their own issues at home.

This was not without its problems and they admitted that they had to catch themselves resorting back to some old strategies; particularly when things got uncomfortable. This was significant because now that their feelings for each other were improved there was more to lose. They admitted that it was difficult, but through catching themselves and through respectfully catching each other, they found they could self-redirect and were able to power through their problems.

It is surprising how powerful this strategy is. I tell clients all the time, "You don't have to go down in the basement and dig up all of the unresolved issues. All you have to do is not throw anything else down there and your relationship will start to heal." This was true of Beth and Carl.

I last saw both of them at a local grocery store, approximately a year after terminating therapy. I tend to be discrete when I see clients outside the office, but I approached them and quietly asked in a knowing tone, "How are things going?" Their response was quick and sincere. Both shook their heads, smiled, and stated "Good."

Chapter Five

GROWING APART

Often when dealing with couples, I use a metaphor of growing apart. I hold my hands together and I tell them, "This was how you felt when you had a sense of being close to each other. When you first started dating, you felt connected, you got your sense of identity from each other, and you got a sense of satisfaction from your relationship." But then as I move my hands away in a V shape, I tell them, "This is what's happening to you. This is how you are growing apart from each other; this is how you are growing alienated from each other."

When couples see this, seeing where they were and then growing apart, it seems to resonate with them. They sense that they are alienated from each other and that they are growing apart rather than growing together. They sense the distance between them. They realize that at one time they got satisfaction from being in the relationship together and being close, but now they are detached from each other.

They sense that something is wrong with the relationship. On occasion, one member of the couple starts to realize just how *alienated* their partner is from them. This is rare because there tends to be a mutual growing apart. However, there

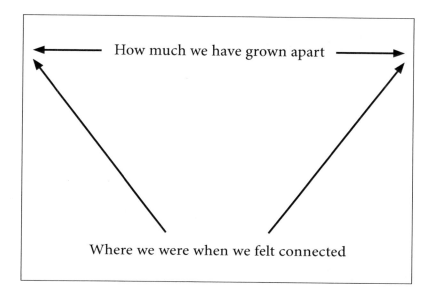

are those rare occasions that one person is ready to leave the relationship and is extremely alienated from their partner. While at the same time, the other partner is pretty happy and does not share their partner's level of resentment and emotional disconnectedness.

The Resentment Rating Scale

One of the main reasons I developed the Resentment Rating Scale was to attribute an actual number for the total amount of resentment to each of the individuals in the couple. Occasionally, one member of the couple has a high number on the scale and their partner has a relatively low number. This is quite rare since usually if there is a high degree of dissatisfaction in the relationship for one individual, there is an equal amount of frustration and alienation for the other. It is a powerful insight when we realize exactly how resentful our partner is with us.

The second benefit of routinely administering the Resentment Rating Scale is that it gives the therapy process a tangible direction. This is something that men in particular seem to appreciate. Not only do you get to list the things that you are frustrated about, but you also get to look at your partner's list. This is powerful because each of the items is given a strength. Items occur along a continuum from something we are not at all resentful about through something that we are extremely bitter about. One would think that after all the arguments that have been survived in the process of a ten-year marriage, each member of the pair would have a good idea of which items would be endorsed and what their number would be. However, nothing could be further from the truth. Couples are routinely surprised by some of the things they think are deal breakers and are rated less powerfully than they expected. They are also taken aback by some of the things that they did not think were significant issues that come up on the scale as generating a good deal of anger or frustration for their partner.

Another way that the Resentment Rating Scale becomes useful is in tracking the success of the therapy process. Changes in the total amount of resentment give the couple hope and show how things have improved. This can also allow for a mid-therapy change in direction, since issues start to be resolved and new ones take on different significance and priority.

The Resentment Rating Scale helps to clarify the things that need to be addressed, it also helps men, in particular, to define and put words to the things that they are angry about. Women in general are more comfortable with articulating their emotions and what is bothering them. This instrument gives men the ability to communicate not only what is bothering them, but also how frustrated they are by it.

The Resentment Rating Scale saves time. The shorter the time in therapy is, the less expensive the process. It allows me, the therapist, to determine in ten or fifteen minutes the source of the couple's problems and gives them confidence that I understand what they are struggling with. Prior to using this instrument, I would have to spend hours (oftentimes painful hours) trying to tease out what exactly it is that members of the couple are angry or resentful about. I don't know how many times one member of the pair has said, "Why didn't you tell me this?" Of course this is consistent with the issue of difficulty with confrontation and the very reason that couples can't or don't get in the ring. A good deal of the time, they don't want the other person to be angry or upset with them.

Name: _____

The Dorman Resentment Rating Scale

5 = Extreme resentment, almost constant anger or frustration

4 = Resentful thoughts on almost a daily basis

3 = Moderate resentment

2 = Occasional frustration or resentment

1 = Minimal resentment

0 = No resentment

_____ 1. Working too many hours, too much focus on work related issues even when home.

_____ 2. Too much focus on friends.

_____ 3. Not enough physical intimacy.

_____ 4. Too much focus on sports or hobbies such as_____.

_____ 5. Too much focus on the children.

_____ 6. Not enough attention.

_____ 7. Treated in a disrespectful manner.

_____ 8. Pressure to perform sexually.

_____ 9. Always angry, anger management issues.

_____ 10. Money management problems, spending money "we don't have."

_____ 11. Parenting problems, disagreement over parenting styles.

_____ 12. Lack of intimacy (i.e., no interest in talking, "I don't feel emotionally connected to you.")

_____ 13. Addiction to gambling, pornography, eating, or _____.

_____ 14. Lack of trust, (i.e., lying).

_____ 15. Infidelity or affair.

_____ 16. Making decisions unilaterally / Not making decisions as a couple.

_____ 17. Inability to resolve differences, lack of conflict resolution skills.

_____ 18. Unfair distribution of chores or work around the house.

_____ 19. "I feel betrayed because when we got married I thought it was going to be different."

_____ 20. Manipulative or controlling, (i.e., things have to be "their way").

_____ 21. 'Bitching', nagging, restating things several times.

_____ 22. Game playing.

_____ 23. Never says what they really want, ("I have to guess what you really want or what's bugging you").

_____ 24. Too passive "I have to make all the decisions" or too assertive "they always have to wear the pants."

_____25. Resentment over the amount of time spent on another "relationship."

_____ 26. _____

_____

_____

_____ Total Points

Chapter Six

WALKING OUT THE DOOR EMOTIONALLY

Once a resentment dynamic has been triggered and it is clear that the couple is unable to settle the differences that would have resolved it, things start to change in the relationship. As I have stated earlier, the level of intimacy deteriorates and the couple feels less connected emotionally. The metaphor that I use to communicate how alienated one or both members of the couple feels, is walking out the door emotionally.

What walking out the door emotionally means is that their minimal level of connectedness has not been met and they no longer feel emotionally close to their partner.

There is a continuum of walking out the door. Stage one is that the individual is unhappy and is walking out the door emotionally. At this stage, individuals often want their partner to come after them and tell them, "Come back in the house." This means that they want their partner to sense that they are no longer in the house with them emotionally and that they will make some changes, "but please come back and let's resolve this." If the other person does not sense they have left the house, this is significant to them because it sends a message about how not in tune their partner is and also how selfish or self- centered the person is. If they really cared, they would be able to tell they were no longer happy and engaging to that person.

If a couple is happy with each other, they get many of their needs met through the relationship. In other words, it fills their cup. The relationship brings them happiness, sexual satisfaction, and a sense of being completed emotionally. When this occurs, people put most of their other interests on the back burner and put more time and energy into the relationship. However, if they are not happy with the relationship or if they are feeling angry and frustrated and emotionally disconnected, are they going to continue to put energy into the relationship?

When we are getting satisfaction from our primary relationship we feed it, we give it time, resources, and our energy. But if it is not giving us anything back or if we start to feel emotionally disconnected from our partner, we start to withdraw ourselves from that relationship. If our relationship does not fill our cup, or leaves us feeling angry, frustrated, or emotionally disconnected, then we start to focus our energies on other activities and relationships. We are drawn back to the kinds of things that scratch our itch for excitement, make us feel successful, or happy. Sometimes, we put energy into the things that give us an escape. This can mean shopping, drinking, or simply getting out of the house to avoid the uncomfortable feelings we have when we are with our partner. We put our energy into the kinds of things that do fill our cup.

When we start to feel like we are failing at one of the most important relationships we have, we tend to try and defend our egos from failure. We focus on the things that make us feel successful or competent. Men tend to focus on such things as their children or their careers. But their hobbies such as golfing, hunting, or friends can start to take their focus away from their relationship with their wife. Women frequently report that they have started to focus their energies more on their children, the house, work, friends, shopping, or working out.

For many people the things that draw them away from the relationship act as escapes or things that for a brief period of time allow them to forget about the stresses of their relationship. Focusing for a few hours on exercising, golfing, shopping, and work all serve to give us a respite away from the pain and drama of our failed relationship. These activities work in the short run, but not in the long run, to help us cope with our pain. In the long run we are only farther away from our mate not closer.

As two people move apart, a void or vacuum starts to be established in the relationship. In fact, these individuals are attempting to scratch an itch or self-medicate with some other satisfying activity because they are no longer getting satisfaction from their primary relationship. When a couple is at this point the things that make them feel successful tend to draw the person *away from the primary relationship;* not back toward it.

These individuals are unhappy (very unhappy), and if they are not pulled back into the relationship, they may move on to stage two: emotionally out the door and around the block. This means that they are one step from filing for divorce. These individuals are often depressed and have lost hope that they will ever be reconnected to their mates. Usually at this stage, little things about the other person bother them and normally they are not interested in physical intimacy. It is not uncommon for the person that is around the block to feel every interaction they have with their spouse leads to an argument and there is very little laughing, joking, or teasing.

At this phase of alienation, other individuals of the opposite sex become more attractive and focus becomes more on our own physical attractiveness.

How much we have grown apart

← Woman   Men →

Woman	Men
Live separate lives	Stay married but live in different worlds
Divorce	Divorce
Sense of indifference	Affair
Feelings of depression	Indifference
Loss of hope	Sense of "I don't care about You"
Find other things to scratch itch, spending, eating, etc.	Easy to be mean
	Feelings of depression
Shopping, martini's with girlfriends	Loss of hope
Cringe when mate touches them	More attempts to hurt wife during arguments
Increase in working out, focus on appearance or less concern about weight	No physical touch/ Not sleeping together
	Almost impossible to resolve differences
Find mate less attractive physically	Decrease in arguing
	Loss of interest in sex
Start to entertain thoughts of other men	Arguing becomes more desperate
	Laughing, joking, and teasing dry up
Nagging and complaining increase	No longer find's mate attractive
Doesn't respond to teasing	No longer responds to mate's attempts at affection
Less Talking	
Loss of interest in physical intimacy	Starts to notice other women/ Responding to or flirting with others
Increased focus on children, job, friends, house	Starts to notice only the things about wife that you don't like (shadow)
Start to let little things about mate bother them	Less concern about weight
	Increase in sarcasm
Arguments become more frequent	Increase in arguing
Arguments are being left unresolved	Starts to focus more on work, golf, friends
	Changes in tone of voice
Nitpicking or voicing complaints	Changes in the way we kiss our wife
	Less talking
Attempt to figure out what is wrong	More difficulty resolving arguments
State of intimacy or connectedness	Initial state of intimacy
Feeling 'In Love'	Feeling "In Love"

Where we were when we felt connected

The third stage of interpersonal alienation is out the door, around the block, and out to the county line. These individuals are at the final phase of separation or estrangement. These individuals are so distant from each other emotionally that they become indifferent, unresponsive, and unsympathetic to the needs of their partner. At this stage, it is easy to be mean to their partner and there is a sense that it is almost impossible to resolve differences. Most people at this phase report they have fallen out of love with their partner.

At this point, many individuals find it easier to simply end their relationships. Occasionally, I will advise a client that it is time to use leverage in order to get their partners attention. By 'leveraging' something, I mean using ultimatums in such a way that the potential positive or negative outcomes are magnified. In other words, a threat; a threat, that if this behavior isn't changed, you will take an action.

Now the risk is this: if an individual is already out to the county line and they barely care about their partner now, why should they take any more risks? They don't want to be hurt any more than they already have been. The act of leveraging something is risky. If they say to their partner, "Hey, you need to spend less time at the office and more time giving me and the kids attention or I am going to file for divorce," there is a risk. The possibility exists that their partner will not change and even though we started to develop hope again, it will be dashed on the rocks; you will be disappointed again. Usually at this point, we have grown distant and hardened. We don't care that much, so why open ourselves to feeling again? If we leverage something like asking them to work less and they are unwilling, won't the person be hurt? Why risk it? And yes, there is the risk that we will be hurt more.

There is the chance, however, that their partner was not aware of how much of a deal breaker the behavior was and now they understand the threat and will make the appropriate changes. Maybe they will realize they have something worth keeping.

How can a person not be aware of how distant their partner is from them? I would say in 70 percent of the cases that I see both people are at approximately the same place. Both are out to the county line and ready to call it quits. In a small portion of the cases, there is either no inkling that their partner is ready to file for divorce or the person has only a slight idea. Sometimes there is such a religious influence in one or both of the individual's lives they never consider that their partner would leave them unless they cheated on them or hit them. I would say that in 10 to 15 percent of the cases I see, one of the individuals is blindsided or shocked to hear that their partner wants a divorce. Most of the time, they don't want out of the relationship and are just guessing at what it is they have to do to make it right.

Most people don't want to make this threat when they are alienated. They don't care anymore. If they still care about their partner, they can be hurt. That is why they need to leverage the behavior *earlier* in the relationship, when they still care; even though this is when they can be hurt the most by their partner's unwillingness to change. If they hear the threat and are still unwilling to change, this is a blow to our egos and how much we thought we meant to our partner. The issue here is when to make your threat and what to do if you make your threat and they call your bluff.

It is usually in this end phase of interpersonal alienation that couples enter marital therapy. That is why the research on couples showing improvement in marital counseling is so poor. The earlier in the relationship you come to therapy, the better the chance there will be improvement. When you come to therapy when you or your partner is out the door and out to the county line emotionally, the chances of saving your relationship go down dramatically.

Often, the act of going into therapy is just that: an act. There is no actual interest in saving the relationship. Rather, it is an attempt to save face and be able to tell family members, "We even tried couples counseling." More often than not, there is a third person involved in the relationship at this time. This of course only complicates the process.

When we start to grow apart from our mate, we feel lonely and that there is a void in our lives. People often find a way to fill this void and make them feel happier and gain some level of satisfaction. They get satisfaction and put energy into the things that *do* give them satisfaction and *do* make them feel successful. As we grow alienated from our partner, people we found attractive to us before now become *really attractive*. Individuals find themselves responding to flattery and flirting in a way they did not when things were happy in their relationship. This becomes something they are now willing to engage in.

What I have found is that women frequently try and fill their lives with their children, their jobs, shopping, jewelry parties, and going out with their girlfriends. Men often fill it with food, increased drinking, pornography, hunting, golfing, or working extra hours. These activities are hollow and tend to work in the short run, but not in the long run to fulfill our needs. As we start to drift further and further apart in our relationship, we find that we become more and more frustrated, more distant, more easily agitated, and more desperate. In general, we become less forgiving of our partner and the things that they do which bug us. Their idiosyncrasies now really get to us. The things that bothered us about them (but we cared about them so much once we over looked them), now seem to be all we see when we look at them. As Dr. Stephen Simmer says, we are now, "In their shadow." By this, he means the shadow of that trait. It is all we see. This starts the process of dehumanizing them and reduces them to only negative traits. This makes it easier to distance ourselves from them and not care for them. It is the process of falling out of love. We overlooked, we forgave, but not anymore. We are walking away from them emotionally.

One last note on walking out the door: it is not uncommon to find clients who prefer to walk out the back door versus the front door. Walking out the front door means that, I am telling you I am unhappy and hoping that this will mean something to you, at least enough to make some changes. Walking out the back door means that emotionally they are at the same place as individuals who are walking out the front door, but their approach is different. When most people take the Resentment Rating Scale, they rate items as 4s or 5s. They are unafraid of their partner's feelings and want them to know how upset they really are with their choices.

Individuals who are walking out the back door take a different approach. When these individuals take the Resentment Rating Scale they mark items with 1s and 2s, maybe a 3. Unlike individuals who are open about their resentment, people who want to sneak out the back door usually have a slightly different attitude toward their partner.

Most of these clients are women. What most of these women say is, "I have a hard time when I get home from marriage counseling with the way he treats me." First, these are typically relationships where one partner wants out and the other does not. Second, there is usually one of two possible dynamics involved. There is either a good deal of guilt induction going on; meaning that if one member of the couple tells the therapist things they are unhappy about, the other feels bad and pouts or makes faces that show they have been hurt. This in turn makes the first person feel bad about complaining. Hence, there is a tendency to not want to communicate the very things that are practically busting out of the person who wants to leave. What do they do with these complaints? It is almost better to keep them inside than to see the look on their partner's face. They don't hate them; they just don't want to live with them anymore. But how do they get out of the relationship?

Another situation I tend to see which makes an individual want to sneak out the 'back door' versus 'the front' is when they are married to either a physically, emotionally, or verbally abusive person. In these situations, **they know** there are going to be implications for their breaking the code of silence. They know that they are going to have a difficult evening if they accurately answer the Resentment Rating Scale and articulate what is truly bothering them. They know that their partner is not going to do a guilt induction, but there will be yelling and screaming (and perhaps more). They want to avoid this; they have suffered through enough evenings of this. They don't want any more. So, these individuals tend to want to take the easy route and sneak out the 'back door'.

What I tell my client's is this: no matter the reason, in the future, you don't want to feel like you left some of the cards on the table. You will want to know that you did whatever you could to save your marriage. This is not the time to walk out the back door. Don't save them the hurt but end the relationship because of your own difficulty in dealing with the other person's pain. Nor should you be bullied into staying.

The answer lays in confronting your partner on how you feel threatened by them. If you need to take some time away from them after a confrontation, then make plans to be away for a day or two until they calm down.

Chapter Seven

How to Finally Solve the Problem

Getting Away From The Blame Game

The first step in the healing process is to get away from the blame game. The blame game is as old as marriage itself. My experience is that most couples play it. They play the game of who is at fault? Who spent too much money this week? Who didn't clean the basement like they said they would? For many, it seems that they realized early on in the relationship that if they could not resolve the arguments they had, they could at least get the satisfaction of laying blame as to who was responsible for the mess. Playing means that each argument is focused not on the behavior that offends you or disrupts the relationship, but rather the behavior that occurred, how long they have been doing it, similar incidents from the past, and what an awful person they are for doing it. The blame game diverts attention from the initial incident and puts the blame on the other person. In other words, the person who feels that they are being attacked turns the table and starts to bring up incidents the other person has done which has not yet been brought to their attention. These include incidents from the other persons past and choices they have made which caused problems in the relationship.

Some time is designated to this reversal and emotions and yelling escalates (all part of the fun of the game). The last part of the blame game involves the punishment phase or time that is usually allotted the person having to pay the price for their behavior. A certain amount of time is designated to making the person pay the price for their choices (otherwise known as enjoy your crime and do your time), and how upset and angry it made them. This involves an intricate and well-thought-out period that is dictated by the offending partner's degree of remorsefulness, guilt, saying they are sorry, or apologizing. During this period of the game, there is a delightful change in the vibe around the household when the person who feels most slighted engages in some form of punishment or guilt inducing behavior. This usually involves the cold shoulder. We refuse to speak to our partner, further nagging or bitching, and in most instances withhold sexual favors.

In the event that the person does not agree to their role in this drama, there are usually other punishments involving refusals to do things around the house or to generally not be around for a period of time. This strategy has a long and honored past despite the fact that it almost never works; hence, the fun of the game. You never know who is going to win, how long the game will take to play, and the general outcome of this spirited match.

Most couples will recognize the blame game and hopefully will laugh when they start to engage in this strategy in the future. What I try to teach couples is an alternative. After I discuss this previous paragraph with them, they see themselves most of the time and how ridiculous their behavior is. Most couples are only guessing at how to resolve their differences.

When you don't have any actual strategies, you come up with what I call home-baked strategies or something we cook up at home; usually something we saw being used when we were growing up.

What I tell couples is that they need to get away from the blaming that does not work and to learn how to *take responsibility for their own behavior.* No diverting attention to some other choice their partner made, no bringing up stuff from the past, no punishing their partner; just taking responsibility for their own roles in how the situation got the way it is.

How do we teach this? The strategy I use is what I call *portioning out the responsibility.* This is a variation of Dr. Stephen Simmer's chips game. What I say is, "If we look at the rug on my floor and this is the entire amount of responsibility for how the situation got the way it is, how much do each of you own? What portion?" I am quick to point out that others call this blame, but we will refer to it as responsibility. I reinforce how the old strategy (bitching, yelling, withholding sex, pointing fingers to make the other person take the blame), isn't working. We need to reframe this situation and concentrate on how they need to stop focusing on making their partner accountable and start taking responsibility for their own roles in how this situation got the way it is; in other words to start taking responsibility for their own behaviors.

I then ask the husband, "If we portion out the responsibility, how much do you have?" I tell them, "I have never seen one person with 100 percent of the responsibility for the situation getting the way it is. So, do you have 50 percent? Is it 60/40? 80/20?" I place a pen on the floor and have him move it around to where he feels his point of responsibility is. I show them how my rug is 100 percent of the responsibility for how the situation got the way it is. I ask, "Are you willing to take responsibility for that portion of the responsibility that lies with you?" I am prone to question a man if he automatically takes half of the blame. This is too easy and reduces the chances that he is truly taking his role seriously. I may say, "But you had an affair and work 60 hours a week!" I then ask, "Do you know what you do that makes up that portion of what you have accepted as your role in this problem?". Most people know the big things that they do, but my experience is that when it comes to the little things, they are only guessing at what it is that is causing resentment and frustration. This is where we revisit the resentment rating scale and look at the things that his wife was resentful about. They are usually all there; his disrespect (a few inches of what he took), his working (a few more inches), etc. Part of the significance of this strategy is for each person to take a portion, **the right portion**, of their responsibility. The other part of this approach that adds power to the intervention comes from a personal understanding of what it is that they do that causes problems in the relationship. What is it that you do that causes problems in the relationship, and are you willing to take responsibility for it? This is a huge insight for most people.

Once the husband has gone through the process of partitioning out his role in the problem, it is much easier to address this with his partner. I am always a little leery of the wife taking whatever portion of the responsibility that is left over. This is rarely the case, and I inform them of this. I tell them, "If you don't feel that you really have 50 percent, don't take it! Only take the portion that you really feel is accurate." Ultimately, she has to look at the choices she is making which make up her role in how things got the way they are. This accountability has to go both ways to be fair. It doesn't work if it isn't sincerely felt that we are taking responsibility for what we really do which is causing problems.

Sometimes not all of the responsibility can be partitioned between two people. Sometimes there is a mother-in-law that is living with the couple and is causing some of the resentment. Sometimes the resentment is due to a particularly difficult child. When this is the case we actually form part of the partition and give it to them; depending on how much each member thinks they deserve.

The power of this intervention is partly in the understanding of what each member of the couple is doing. Even the little things they are doing that causes resentment. Each of these little things counts as an inch on the floor. *A number of little things can build up!* Don't dismiss them. My experience is that most people want to know what it is they are doing that causes their partner to withdraw, as long as they have a strategy for effectively dealing with the problem.

When portioning out the responsibility has been completed, we move on to the part which involves changing our proportion of the responsibility. This involves going home and making some adjustments to our behavior. What I often see is reluctance on the part of either partner to make a large number of changes. Usually, after it is made clear that pointing fingers doesn't work, there is a realization that true change is going to have to start at home, by taking responsibility for their own portion of the problem. As they realize this is true, most people work on changing one or two things that they do. Not wholesale changes, not totally being the person their partner wants them to be, but a few changes. Then, most people sit back and see if their changes are making any difference in the way their partner is treating them. *Is their partner making any changes in their own behaviors?* Once we see that this strategy is working, we tend to be willing to continue on to bigger issues; requiring more difficult changes. This strategy usually involves each person working on their own issues and then as they are successful with those, their partner makes a few of their own. Usually, they match their own investment in changing to their partner's.

It is important at this point to reinforce the changes each person sees their partner making. However, it is normal to say, "I recognize that you are making some changes, BUT..." It is important to fight your impulse to say, "BUT." This doesn't help. It only makes people defensive and undoes whatever healing and hope they have developed. When we don't take small changes as successes, it makes people feel that their partner will never be happy. They will say to themselves, "They don't see what I am doing. I can't make them happy anyway. All they see is what I am not doing. I don't even want to try."

Part of the partitioning game is dividing out the portion of behaviors you engage in which cause problems; that part of the responsibility you are willing to take for how the situation got the way it is. Are you aware of what you are doing that is causing problems in the relationship or within the family? This is significant because without understanding what *we* are doing, the focus is probably going to continue to be on our mate and *their* behaviors; the things they are doing that are continuing to make us angry and resentful. This is the same old dynamic that most couples and families have been engaging in for years. Does it work? Does looking at your mate's behaviors and expecting them to take responsibility change the feelings that you have for them? Probably not. What are the things you are doing that are causing problems and resentment? Most couples have a difficult time getting away from the blame game. They are reluctant to try something new. Initially, when they make changes, they are bound to be small. I like to encourage them to make some changes that are visible or apparent when they are changed. I also like to go for something that on the Resentment Rating Scale was a 4 or a 5; something that has historically caused resentment. When your mate works on something you view as a deal breaker, it says that they want to work things out and make your relationship better. They aren't working on a minor problem and hope you will work on a big one. It is simply saying, "I am not focused on you and your behavior right now. I am going to focus on me and my role in causing problems in this relationship." Even if the partitioning of the responsibility has been completed and the results were 90/10, that you only have 10 percent of the responsibility for the relationship getting the way it is; you are going to work on your own problem and let your mate work on theirs. Most couples are quite alienated emotionally at this point. Don't expect big changes. Expect small changes.

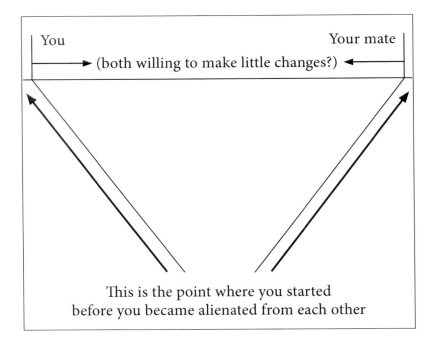

Once small changes have been made and a period of time has gone by, most couples stop and take a look at the situation. Is there evidence that these changes are integrated? Are they real and part of the way the person is now behaving? Are they permanent, or are they going back to the way that you used to behave? These questions must be answered before the couple can go on to stage two.

In the next step, more changes are made. In the first stage, each member of the couple was testing the other to see if they would make changes and would those changes be real, or would they be either just for show or short-lived. Once each member of the couple has been convinced that this new strategy may have some credibility, they continue to work this approach and try and see if maybe this tactic will work, because their home-baked plan sure hasn't.

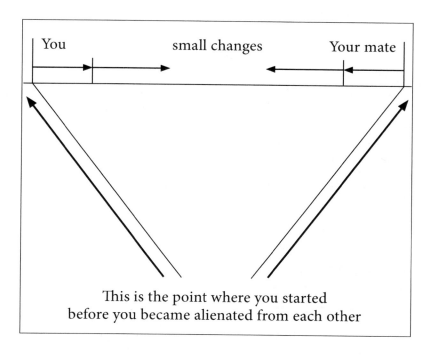

You | small changes | Your mate

This is the point where you started
before you became alienated from each other

Once it has been established that each partner has to take responsibility for their own behaviors, it will become clear that this strategy is working. Each side is simply focused on their own role, their own portion of the partition. There is no more pointing of fingers at the other. When this transition takes place, something happens: our *perceptions* of the other starts to change. We are seen as more approachable. We are actually working on this together. We are seen as more **grown-up or mature.** We now actually start to have hope that we may be able to regain some of the emotional connection that we have lost in the process of becoming alienated from each other; these changes and the insights that come with them free us up to make even greater changes in our behavior.

As you can see from the diagram above, once the initial small changes have borne fruit, larger changes can now be risked. This is where real growth and forgiveness happens. This is where we see how good it can get. Does the couple find a way to make it 50 percent back to normal or pre-alienation levels of connection? Can they make it all the way back or even find greater levels of connection? Can this relationship be better than it was even at the start? The answer to these questions is YES!

I don't know how many couples have said on our last session, "We are happier than we have ever been." It is wonderful as a therapist to see a couple look at each other in a way that communicates love and respect versus the contempt and disgust that I saw in their eyes only five or six short weeks ago. I often ask the question, "How can it be that for the majority of people there was more trust, caring, and self-disclosure in their relationship after two months of dating than after twenty years of marriage?" Your relationship has a chance to catch-up and to have the degree of intimacy and connection that it should have. For all the years that most couples have been together there should be some connection to associate with it. Instead of the early years being just happiness based on brain chemistry and neurotransmitters, this new relationship has the chance to be genuine and based on reality as opposed to the feel good, fantasy world of courting and dating.

I have spent the first part of this book talking about how important it is to be emotionally connected to our mates. I have also made a case for why we have to be able to resolve our differences and not allow them to be thrown into the basement to ferment and affect the intimacy level of our relationship.

So how does this all get resolved? What are the strategies that I teach couples which let them take this from an insight level to a practical level? Insight is the easy part. This, dear reader, is where it starts to get hard.

Chapter Eight

GETTING IN THE RING/STAYING IN THE RING

The first thing that a couple has to learn to improve their relationship is to figure out how to get in the ring and stay in the ring until their problems are solved. The ring is a metaphor for that place where every couple needs to go to resolve their issues. In essence, it is how a couple agrees to argue. Some people are very comfortable getting into the ring and realize that it is a necessary part of defining roles within a relationship; determining who will do what chores and how various differences of opinion will be settled. Conflict, especially with someone we care about and want approval from, can be extremely difficult. One of the biggest problems I see in couples is the *inability to tolerate the awkwardness and uncomfortableness of arguing.* Fifty percent of the time, this means a discussion and 50 percent of the time this means an argument. The longer you go without resolving your differences, the better the chance that if there is some issue in your lives it will end in an argument versus a discussion.

Arguing or discussing important issues within a relationship makes most people uncomfortable; this sense of our partner being upset with us is unpleasant. What do most people do when faced with something that they don't want to do or something that is unpleasant? Often, when people don't want to engage in these uncomfortable and awkward discussions, they flee from them, citing their discomfort and anxiety. In essence, "I don't like to argue with you, so I won't." *The great irony is that in avoiding these arguments to save our relationship, we end up damaging it by not doing so.*

At a practical level, if there is an issue (for example, money, parenting, sex, golfing, the in-laws) and if a couple is willing to get in the ring and discuss or argue about the issue and reach a compromise, they get an outcome both can live with. If they are mature enough or have the compromising skills to resolve the issues, (and to a greater extent) the ability to tolerate the discomfort and awkwardness that comes when couple's disagree, they usually resolve or solve their problem. Not only do couples need to learn the techniques of staying calm, asking for what they want in clear and observable ways, but also how to fight in ways that are fair and civil.

Often, couples do a fairly decent job of getting in the ring and discussing the issue. The thing I see most often as a therapist is that they discuss it and both sides know what the other wants. What they don't do is go the final step.

The final step is getting the closure they need to put the issue to rest. This means asking, "So, what's the plan?" What did we agree on or where is the compromise that we can both live with? Did we fully paint the picture of what we want the situation to look like in the future? There is an old tactic in sales; that is asking for the sale. Literally, how many can I put you down for or will you agree to buy this product? In many ways, agreements at the end of being in the ring are like this: We can discuss things ad nauseum, but if we don't add that final step (when we have to compromise or agree to something that we don't want to) we will never keep the issue out of the basement. Some couples find that a great strategy is for one of them to start this final process by stating "I propose..." This is a great approach because it gives a couple a starting point. Maybe they are not that far apart after all. We have a bid, a proposal. Some people may accept the offer if it is fair. If not, at least the other person has an idea of where their partner wants to be. We stay in the ring and make a counter offer or continue the argument (making a statement such as, "You've got to be kidding," or something that leads to more issues in the basement and fewer resolved). Remember, relationships take compromising and maturity. Ask yourself, are you better off getting your way all the time or being happy?

Whether you use this strategy or not, after some discussion someone has to say, "So what did we agree to? Or what's the plan?" Other couples ask, "What is the win-win here, do we have to write it down or is your word enough?"

How Well Do You Stay In The Ring?

- How does arguing with your mate make you feel?
- Does it bring back memories of your past, when you were a child?
- Does it tap into forgotten memories of your parent's marriage or how they disrupted the house with their arguing?
- Does your arguing style make you feel disrespected? Bullied? Uncomfortable? Why?
- Does your partner make you feel heard? Respected?
- Do they push your buttons?

- Do you fear the repercussions?
- Are you reluctant to argue with your mate because you are afraid that they won't let you back in the marital bed for a week? Will they not speak to you for a day or two?
- Is your physical safety at risk and do you have fears that your partner will become physically abusive with you? Does this fear keep you from saying what you want to say?
- Is this really something that your partner would do or is it a residual emotion left over from a past relationship? Was there a past partner who would intimidate, physically strike, or hurt you?
- How do we respond when our partner argues with us? Do we place them on extinction and give them no eye contact or act as though they were not there?
- Are *we* sabotaging our partner's ability to come to us and bring up issues that are bothering them? Have we looked in the mirror at our own role in our partner's inability to come to the table or get in the ring?
- Do we intimidate? Do we do guilt inductions?
- Do the words become so hurtful that we no longer focus on the issue but on hurting our partner?
- Do we revert back to age-old strategies of bringing up problems from the past or name-calling?
- Do we withhold sex or withhold "us," to get our partner's to be compliant and not complain? We have a good thing going and don't want to change it?

All of these questions have to be asked in order to better understand what keeps us from successfully resolving our issues or disagreements.

What are Your Barriers to Conflict Resolution?

I developed the questionnaire **Barriers to Resolving Conflict** in order for couples to be able to look at their own role and the role of their partner in resolving conflicts. This is the questionnaire that I give couples. Usually, I give this to them after we have fully discussed the issues on the Resentment Rating Scale.

Name_____

Barriers to Resolving Conflict

Instructions: Think about what typically happens during an argument. Place a check in front of the things your partner does that derail the argument for you or make you not want to continue (example: yells at me, brings up things from the past). At the end of the exercise list the top three things that derail an argument (example: 4, 10,18).

- ☐ 1. Point fingers at each other (figuratively or physically?).
- ☐ 2. Partner seems more interested in trying to hurt me with words rather than resolving the problem.
- ☐ 3. Perceived untruthfulness (meaning, I think they are lying).
- ☐ 4. Brings up issues from the past.
- ☐ 5. I stopped because it felt like they were getting angry with me.
- ☐ 6. Unable to stay on the topic of conflict, going down some other path.
- ☐ 7. Yelling/swearing.
- ☐ 8. Feel threatened/intimidated.
- ☐ 9. Partner gets defensive and states, "Well, you do this."

☐ 10. Partner states, "Why don't we just get a divorce then?"

☐ 11. I can't believe them. They have said this before and never held their end of the bargain.

☐ 12. Partner performed a guilt induction to make me feel bad.

☐ 13. Partner interrupted me.

☐ 14. Partner talked in a disrespectful tone or made faces that were disrespectful.

☐ 15. Partner leaves/gives up too easily.

☐ 16. Talks to me like a child or like I am stupid.

☐ 17. Agrees with me so they can escape/avoid the conflict.

☐ 18. Rolls their eyes.

☐ 19. Says, "Never mind. You're right, I am always wrong."

☐ 20. Afraid to wake up the kids/argue in front of children.

☐ 21. Stops because partner started to cry.

☐ 22. Gives up too easily.

☐ 23. Fill in your own example if not listed above. _____

_____

_____

List the top three barriers that derail an argument for you:

1. _____

2. _____

3. _____

Chapter Nine

THE KEYS
TO RESENTMENT
REDUCTION

What I am suggesting in this book is that there needs to be a paradigm shift in how we treat couples with damaged interpersonal relationships. Historically, the focus has been on improving communication skills. While important, I do not believe this is the key to improving marital relationships. The key to improving one's relationship has to do with understanding the barriers that individuals have in staying in the ring. Learning how to stay in the ring and fully discuss their problems is a HUGE issue for most couples.

When individuals take responsibility for their own issues in a relationship rather than focus on their partner's, the chances of resolving their problems goes up dramatically. Likewise, when each person in the relationship looks at their own difficulty in getting in, or perhaps more importantly staying in the ring, long lasting improvements can be made. We have to look at our own barriers; those things that keep **_us_** from staying in the ring and getting closure on our problems. We have to get our own house in order.

The Barriers to Resolving Conflict questionnaire is not a complete list of all of the possible problems. Every couple is unique and has their own list of reasons for why they don't complete their arguments. Is it that one person rolls their eyes disrespectfully? This taps into their partner's reservoir of anger at being disrespected in past relationships. Do they then become angry too quickly and start to fight dirty? Do they bring up every issue that the couple has had to deal with over the last ten years and rehash it in order to make their partner feel like scum? (This is an almost classic dynamic.)

By going down the list and checking off what problems each person sees, they take responsibility not only for their own conflict avoidance problems but also checkoff the problems they feel their partner brings to the ring. This is powerful because oftentimes people have a blind spot and do not see their own role in problems being left in the basement. One would think that ten years of arguing by a couple would bring a good deal of insight to both parties about what each does that causes problems. Nothing could be further from the truth. Each person sharing their list with their partner and then articulating their problems, starts to paint a picture of what an argument has historically looked like for a couple.

Only when individuals see their own barriers are they able to overcome them. Sometimes this is relatively easy. Usually, coming to an insight or awareness of what they do to shutdown discussions is enough to help a couple. However, there needs to be individual sessions for one or both members of the couple to better help them understand the nature of their resistance; where it came from and how it affects their partner when they use it.

Communication can only get a couple so far on the road to problem resolution. The problem is to get closure or total understanding about a problem and then solving the disagreement. In order to do this, a couple must power through their barriers and learn to tolerate their discomfort.

Do You Know How To Negotiate?

Do you get what you deserve or do you get what you negotiate. As our relationships develop and mature, we need to have the tools in our toolbox to handle differences. We need to be willing to take drastic (and sometimes difficult) measures to get what we deserve. You have to be able to negotiate!

Happiness discriminates against the fearful and the nonassertive. In the past, there was no need to negotiate what got done around the house. Men did the cars, the lawn, the heavy lifting, and the providing. Women took care of the children, cooked meals, and cared for the house. Sounds absurd, doesn't it?

Things have changed so much in today's families. There are no hard-and-fast rules today about who should do what. This is both a good thing and a bad thing. It is good because it teaches our children that they need to be responsible for the house; not the traditional male chores or the traditional female chores; just the chores. You now get to do the things you enjoy doing. If you enjoy cooking (as I do), then why not take cooking and let your mate take some other task. The problem with this is that almost *everything now has to be negotiated*. There are no understandings about who does what. We have to get in the ring and agree on who is going to do what. This can be great or it can open up a great deal of resentment. If you are good at negotiating, you will get a fair share of the work (and more than likely) the tasks you enjoy doing. However, if you are passive or not good at negotiating then what you agree to do might leave you angry, resentful, and overwhelmed with an unfair load of the household chores.

To negotiate means looking at a problem, deciding how much you agree on, and trying to find a solution that you can both live with. Yes, neither will get what they wanted as their first choice, but that is the nature of long-term relationships. So how do you compromise?

First, it is important to be able to brainstorm, meaning being able to throw out all of the possible options. Resist the temptation to retreat when your partner throws out options that seem only in their best interest. This is where communication skills come into play. Be patient. Get all of the options on the table. Now that you have a list of what each of you wants, it is important to take a critical look at all of the options. Are some of your partner's options actually good ideas? Will some of them work? Who won the last argument or got their way the last time? If it was you, then your partner may be expecting you to move a little closer toward the way they want the decision to go this time. Compromise is the name of the game. Compromise is important to a couple, because it gives them hope.

Now that you have all of the possible scenarios out on the table, don't be afraid to ask for a deal. Look for something in the middle ground or slightly in your best interest. Anything too close to what you initially wanted will either end up with a smile (meaning nice try) or your partner getting frustrated and potentially giving up. You are better off looking mature and giving your partner some of the things they wanted. Ultimately, one of you needs to ask, "So what is the plan?" or "What did we agree on?" I also like, "Here is what I propose," as ways to get the ball started in the closure phase of a negotiation.

Words of wisdom here: I know that it feels weak sometimes to give in; to let your partner get more than you feel they deserve. That is OK; it takes strength to make this choice. Ask yourself, "Am I better off being happy or right? Am I better off making my partner feel good about the agreement and giving them hope or getting my way?"

Learning How to Resolve Your Differences and Improve Your Relationship

You have read about the place where unresolved issues go. You have visualized in your mind's eye the shape of a resentment dynamic and came to an understanding about what initially served as a trigger. You have come to an understanding of what maintained it and where it has ultimately led your relationship. If you are like most couples, you have agreed that you are perhaps not as bad a match as you started to believe. If you could resolve your differences, you could reduce the resentment and regain a sense of connectedness. If you believe in the resentment dynamic theory of emotional alienation, you have probably also worked on what a traditional argument looks like for you. Ultimately, it is what keeps you from getting in the ring or staying in the ring to get closure. Now what do you do? What is the next step in restoring your relationship to one that is characterized by teasing, laughing, and increased physical intimacy?

First–stop complaining, criticizing, doing guilt inductions, or withholding love or sex to get what you want. Try asking for what you want in a clear, specific, and positive manner. It is also important to start these discussions by expressing appreciation for the positive things your partner does for you and the relationship. **Some things we work through; some things we get over.** If she is a night owl, she is never going to come to bed with you. If he wants to go to deer camp for a week, aren't you better off letting him go and skipping the argument for the rest of the year? You need to pick your battles. Pick the ones that mean the most to you. Otherwise, you win the battle but lose the war and appear controlling and parental.

The key here is to ask for what you want in clear, specific terms. Don't say, "The house sure is dirty." Try, "Can you vacuum when I am gone?"

Second, try and see things from their point of view. I know that this seems naive, but sometimes we get so focused on having things our way that we view the world only through our own goggles. We have lost the ability to believe that there are other ways of seeing things which may be as valid as our own. Plus, looking at things the way our partners do and communicating this sends a strong message about trying to be open-minded.

Third, state your case clearly and use specific examples. Do not use universal statements such as, "You always do this" or "This happens every time." Describe specific instances and how you felt when it occurred. Most people respond well to specifics; hinting, intimating, and making innuendos don't work with most people. Just say what is bothering you, but do so in a practiced, rehearsed, and respectful way.

Fourth, avoid personal attacks. It is natural to become angry during arguments, but don't fall into the trap of calling your partner names or trying to hurt them. Doing so will not only cause more resentment but also decreases the hope that things can be resolved.

Fifth, pick an appropriate place to have a discussion. Don't argue in public or when children are around. Also, pick a moment when you have enough time to reasonably come to a resolution.

Sixth, if the person apologizes and says they'll work on it, give them enough time to do that. Don't expect your partner to make significant changes without some backsliding and reverting to prior ways of doing business. What I frequently tell clients is, "The line from where you are to where you want to be is not a straight line." The improvement line has good days and bad days. It takes patience to see the improvement; no matter how gradual. It is also important to ask the person, "How do you want me to tell you if things are going bad or if I see you going back to the way you were?" If the offending behavior continues, remind them in the way they recommended. Once again, keep your anger in check and point out specific behaviors that have shown improvement. It is important not to bring up old arguments. Focus on the present. It is better to say, "You remember when I asked how you wanted me to tell you when you were going back to the way you used to be? Well…"

Seventh, fake it till you make it. Sometimes we have to be the bigger person and be the first one to make changes. I know we don't always feel like being the first to make changes, but sometimes we take the lead and make the change first and then our partners see that we have made some good faith efforts. They make changes of their own. Sometimes, we show softness when communicating and look at our partner when talking to them. We may not be sincere the first few times we soften our voice. It wouldn't be the first time that after we change the way we respond to them, they change the way they respond to us. Sometimes we fake it until it becomes the way we sincerely do business.

Chapter Ten

Understanding the Rules of Engagement for Constructive Arguing

Understanding the rules for constructive arguing is an important element in increasing the chances that you will resolve your problems. How couples argue varies greatly. Some couples get loud, some get disrespectful, some aim for a sense of, "I am the parent and you are the child." Whatever the typical argument strategy, there are things to remember that increase the chances for a couple to get in the ring and stay in the ring.

Couples need to remember that the more intense the emotions, the better the chance one or both individuals will get out of the ring. The more intense the emotions, the greater the chance that someone will say something so hurtful that the argument no longer stays focused on the issue that was initially to be discussed. Now it becomes focused on the argument itself and in many instances hurting the other or laying blame.

Keeping this in mind, it is important to understand that emotion management (essentially being aware of how heated the argument is getting) is important. I ask my clients to visualize a starting point. I call this calm. This is usually my hand in a horizontal position. Then, I increase the intensity of the interaction and raise my hand a bit. This is on edge, then tense, then agitated. I raise my hand even more. After agitated is angry, then extremely angry, and finally, inflamed. Inflamed is where my hand is at almost a 90 degree angle. (NOTE: I made the phrases used match what was on the chart.)

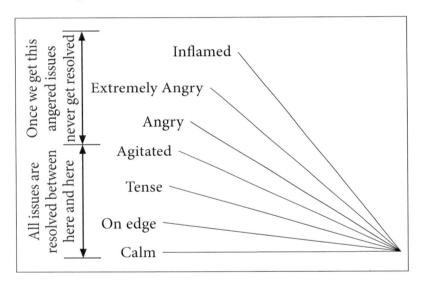

All issues in the history of the world were resolved between calm and agitated. Nothing gets resolved once we are angry.

When we argue, it is important to be aware of how angry the words are becoming. We need to be aware of the intensity, the volume, and the looks on each other's faces. It is important to understand where each individual is emotionally during an argument. The reason is simple: *arguments never get resolved once emotions get past the angry phase.*

This is why we have to be aware of the kind of things that escalate emotions within an argument. Essentially, most couples come to a Y in the road. Do they discuss the issue civilly, do they hurt each other with words, do they try and lay blame, or do they try and resolve the issue? Individuals have to stay exquisitely aware of each other's emotions. More importantly, it means understanding the kind of things that push our partner's buttons and accelerates their anger. When couples are conscious of their emotions and understand what strategies they typically use when arguing, they can be aware of when they are becoming too angry to resolve their problems and when they are slipping back into their old default mode of doing business.

Here are some strategies for increasing the chances that you and your partner will successfully resolve the next issue that you argue over.

Take Time-Outs If the Argument Gets Too Heated

Time-out's are powerful strategies; taking time away from the situation or the other person when things get too intense is a good strategy. This keeps emotions from getting too powerful or anger from boiling over. Where there is anger and the actual threat of harm, we are worried about our health and safety. This leads to not resolving the conflict. If you find yourself getting so angry that you might hurt someone or say something that might really damage the relationship, take a time-out. If you find yourself being so angry that you can't concentrate or think straight, take a time-out. There is no weakness in taking some time to collect ourselves and get our emotions under control. Nothing shuts down discussions quicker than the sense that this could escalate into something really intense or dangerous.

When you take a time-out, do so wisely. Don't take this opportunity to inflame yourself further. Try to talk yourself down. Know how long it takes to really calm down. Don't let yourself get talked into a timeline, come back in a half-an-hour for example. Some people, once angry, take up to a day to calm down.

When you take a time-out, go to your basement or garage. Go outside or to your bedroom. Distract yourself with some other activity that you enjoy. Don't consume alcohol or leave the home. Try to stay close to your mate, but out of their view.

Here is the problem I frequently see with people taking time-outs. For example, a man becomes uncomfortable or feels his anger is rising to the point of possibly losing his temper and striking out. If he has fears that he will say something that will damage the relationship, he should take a time-out.

Now the problem is not that he is taking a time-out. He should go to the garage or the basement and cool down. The problem occurs when he has taken a time- out and it has worked. She didn't follow him to the basement. She let him have some space. He now comes to a point where he has to make a decision. He walks back in the house and listens. It is quiet. So, he can choose option number one: walk back in like nothing happened. After all, quiet was what he wanted. He can stay under her radar and act like nothing happened. Or, he can choose option number two: walk back in after calming down enough to be civil and have a productive discussion and say, "Where did we leave off?"

The problem is that if we don't like conflict and get a chance to avoid it, we usually do. The mark of a mature person is that they can go back to address something they don't want to deal with. By coming back, we show maturity and give our partners hope that we can deal with whatever life throws at us. What

I see time and time again is that one of the partners takes a time-out and then sneaks back in the house acting like nothing happened, then the next time they try to take a time-out to calm down, their partner says, "Oh, no, not this time, you are not going to avoid it this time." They follow you out to the garage or the basement and get in your face and maybe into a corner with their finger in your chest. What happens now? You know the answer; angry and cornered. That is a recipe for disaster.

So remember, take the time-out if you are getting too angry to be productive, but don't avoid the problem. You will only save it up for another time and be seen as immature. Be wise and deal with the situation. No excuses, no avoidance.

Don't Call Each Other Names or Swear

It is easy when in the heat of an argument to hurt each other with words. It's easy to choose words like, 'C#*T', 'Bastard' or 'Bitch.' We know that these words hurt people. We see the look in their eyes when we use them. These are cheap shots. They are immature and meant to hurt, not to constructively work on the relationship. When we get hurt, we want to hurt back. Nothing hurts as effectively or as quickly as calling someone a bitch or an A@#hole. Many people state that they would rather be physically hit than to be emotionally hurt the way that swearing hurts them. Avoid swearing at each other. Remember, you're better off stopping at the point that swearing starts because, as I tell my clients, *"once you start swearing nothing is going to get resolved!"*

Don't Point Fingers at Each Other

There are two types of pointing fingers. The first is physically pointing our fingers at our mates. The second is symbolically 'pointing our fingers' or laying blame on our partner even though we never physically do this. When we point fingers at each other, there is a natural response to see your spouse as the reason for the problem. The result is they get defensive. Pointing fingers has a tendency to raise the level of agitation in an already uptight situation. Pointing fingers is inflammatory. Try extending your hand with the palm up. This way you are perceived as offering something to your spouse rather than blaming them.

Throwing Out The "D" Word

Few things reduce the chances of resolving an issue as much as reaching for the phrase "then why don't we just get a divorce". By threatening divorce, we are sending the message that we have such little hope of resolving the argument and that we have so little interest in keeping the relationship, we might as well give up. It is easy when angry, to propose a divorce, it hurts, it threatens the other to stand down or I will follow through on my warning. But it is important when we are looking at our own role in our arguments to be aware of our tendency to reach for this. Easy yes, but resist the temptation and stay in the ring and focus not on hurting your mate but on decreasing the anger and level of intensity.

Don't Say Things Like "Never Mind, You're Always Right, or I Am Always Wrong"

We say, "You're always right. I am always wrong," in two different ways; both to make a point. The first way we say it is in a sarcastic manner. How ridiculous to believe that you are always right in every situation and that I am always wrong. In this situation we are saying that when we argue, it feels like you are always right and I am always the one who has made a mistake. The sarcasm is palpable. Sarcasm rarely works in the long run to help resolve differences.

The second way is in the hangdog: "No, no, you're right, I messed up again," sort of way. Once again, this is not helpful because it doesn't take responsibility for the problem in a sincere way. This is the, "If I just admit that I was wrong, you will minimize your nagging" approach. I want this to last as short as possible. So, if I admit that I was wrong, whether I believe I was wrong or not, you will stop your arguing quicker. Once again, this doesn't work in the long run.

Don't Scream or Yell

Yelling feels good; it allows us to vent our frustration and anger and show our mate how passionate we are about the situation. However, yelling has the effect of escalating the emotions of a situation. When things get too uncomfortable, staying in the ring gets harder and some partners flee. To decrease the chances of this, keep things quieter. Try to talk in moderate, civil tones. This doesn't feel as good, but it increases the chance that things will stay civil and that you will get the resolution you want. No one hears words that are screamed.

Nothing is shouted louder than what you say in hushed tones. Hushed tones are a sure message that you are serious. No yelling, no screaming. You are just telling them what they need to hear. This is a more effective strategy than screaming.

Don't Interrupt Each Other

Interrupting our partner is one of the easiest ways to show disrespect and send a message that, "My message is more important than yours." It takes maturity and self-control to not interrupt, but the payoffs are huge. It takes self-control and maturity to let your partner talk. Take the high road and let them vent. And listen! Let them know that you are listening. Nod, say OK, and maintain eye contact. When they come up for breath, ask, "Now can I have my say?" This is more effective than interrupting and sends a message about one's maturity and interest in truly dealing with the issues.

Don't Bring Up Issues from The Past

It is natural to try and make a case for ourselves to show why we are so upset with our partners. This usually involves bringing up other cases from the past when they disappointed us in similar ways. The problem with this strategy is that it causes problems. Yes, it works to make a strong case that your spouse has a history of engaging in the same behavior in the past and that it has caused resentment. The problem is that it is interpreted as dredging up all your partner's old mistakes and makes them feel like they are children and you are the parent. This shuts down communication rather than encourages it. Focus on the situation at hand; the one problem that you are trying to resolve today. Chances are the person who you are upset with knows how long they have been doing this behavior and they don't need to be reminded and embarrassed any more than they already are.

Don't Roll Your Eyes or Make Faces

Rolling of eyes, whether it is by our children or our mate, communicates the same thing; "You are so stupid." Few things elicit anger as much as people rolling their eyes at us. In the process of working through an individual's anger, we frequently discuss the kinds of things that make them defensive or angry.

Once established, we call these situations our buttons. Now buttons can be an individual feeling embarrassed, or the sense that people are hinting that they are not smart, etc. By far, the most common button I hear people report is the sense of being disrespected. Disrespect angers people faster than just about anything. Rolling one's eyes is one of the easiest ways to show someone disrespect.

Don't Say Things Like "Whatever"

When we say, "whatever," we are dismissing the person we are arguing with. We think that we are simply refusing to be drawn in to the same old argument, but for them it feels like we have chosen this phrase to check out of the argument and walk away. Saying "whatever" is never followed by anything constructive or a statement that suggests someone wants to continue this disagreement.

Don't Go Down the Paths That Lead
To Some Other Issue

In the process of doing couples therapy, I get to listen to a lot of couples argue. They try to be civil at first, but ultimately they can't stand it and revert back to their old arguing style. I get to hear in the comfort of my own office what it sounds like in their front room. What I hear a good deal of the time is a couple switching topics. They start arguing about issue A (perhaps money) and end up bringing up issues B, C, and D (in-laws, parenting, and chores). Do they ever get in the ring and get closure on any one problem? Almost never. By bringing up so many other issues, it virtually eliminates any chance that they will get a resolution to their problem. What typically happens is that they get off-track or distracted by some other issue they also had resentment about and brought up that problem. They both go on to discuss that issue (or another issue is brought up.) They ended up nowhere close to the issue they started with but ran out of emotional energy and stopped. So that is where they ended. They left the problem unresolved.

Listen to yourselves argue. If you are one of the many couples that starts out at one place and ends up at another, you may need to be aware of the need to focus. I know that it is hard. Once feelings have been hurt and tempers flare, it is easy to bring up all of the other hurts; all of the other examples of your partner's mistakes. Avoid the temptation to bring up several other issues (most warrant being their own argument or discussion anyway). Stay on topic. If you have to be the one that says, "We are getting off the topic" or "Let's just keep discussing this issue," so be it.

Don't Say Yes, But...

There is a tendency, and we have all succumbed to it, when in a heated argument saying, "Yes, but." Saying "Yes, but," feels to your partner like you just dismissed everything they just said. If we have just confronted our partner about a number of things that we are angry about, and then we hear them say "yes, but," it feels like they just discounted everything we just said, or it feels like they are being defensive. Avoid this when arguing. Accept what your partner is saying. Lean into it, don't dismiss it, or deflect it. Hear it. Say yes, I hear what you are saying. You are saying...

Don't Get in Your Partners Personal Space

One of the things I frequently tell my couples is that something happens as soon as people get in our personal space (as soon as they stand up and lean in and get in our face). When this happens, we have taken the discussion to a whole different level. Are we going to resolve this disagreement now? Once someone gets to this point in an argument, things never get resolved. We sometimes say things to get out of the argument or shut them down, but long-term strategies for dealing with our disagreements never come from these types of engagements. What does come from these types of encounters is a physical escalation or sense of being bullied. Resist the temptation to get in your partner's personal space. Give them at least three feet or more of space between you and them if you want to improve the chances of the problem being resolved.

Don't Get Defensive

It's tempting, when arguing to put blame on our partners versus taking responsibility for ourselves. I don't know how many clients have said, "As soon as I say, you didn't keep your bargain regarding how much you were going to spend." Their partners, rather than admit they went over their budget and commit to do better (what you wanted them to say) , became defensive and stated, "Yea, but you didn't clean up the garage like you said you would." This is frustrating because it perpetuates the blame game and keeps couples from resolving the main issue. Couples need to be willing to take responsibility for their own mistakes and not resort to distracting the focus from themselves onto their partner's mistake. If they are truly upset with their partner, they need to select another time to address that issue. If it is not significant enough to address on its own, it is probably not significant enough to bring up in the first place. The lesson here is this. Don't get defensive and say, "Well you do this". The lesson is also that if there is something that you want to bring up about your partner's behavior, wait don't broach it in the middle and an argument. If it is significant enough to address, give it the focus it deserves and bring it up as its own discussion, not as an aside or as a strategy to deflect attention from your own mistake.

Use Empathic Listening

The premise of empathic listening is that one tries to understand another person's point of view and to communicate to them that they have heard and gotten what was trying to be said. I know a lot of people who say, " I heard what she was saying, I got it the first time she said it." The problem with this is that unless the other person knows that you heard what they were saying, there is a tendency to get stuck in a certain area of discussion. This is so important; I am going to say it again: we tend to get stuck at one point in our discussion or argument, if our partners are not convinced that we heard what they were saying. In order to move on in the discussion, we have to communicate that we understand not only what they were saying (their point of view) but *the emotional component as well.* There needs to be two important elements met. In order to move on and not be paralyzed, we have to feel that our partner understands what we are experiencing and the emotions that this brings up, the emotional component.

How understanding does a person feel if you say to them, "I know, I know" during an argument? Not very. How understood do they feel, however, if we use empathic listening and communicate both what they are experiencing and the emotions that they are feeling? For example: "I know that you were disappointed (the emotional component) when you found out that I had made plans to go out of town for a workshop without consulting you" (the situation).

So how does empathic listening work? The first thing that communicates that we are listening to our spouse is to look at them. This means appropriate eye contact, not staring at them. I know a lot of men in particular who say, "I can read the paper and still hear what she is saying." The issue isn't whether you can hear your spouse; the point is that you are stopping what you were doing because it was important for you to hear your spouse. It is also important to be aware of your body posture. Are you leaning forward slightly with your arms crossed in front of you? This is a closed posture and suggests defensiveness. Try and open up your posture a bit. Are you stiff or are you silently nodding your head in to communicate that you are hearing what they are saying, especially at significant points?

Now, it is important to communicate that we are not in a hurry for them to get to the point. This means that we have to communicate that we want them to continue and give them permission to deepen their level of communication. We do this by saying things like, "right," "OK," or "I know." It is extremely important at this point when you have your spouse communicating to not shut down this process. This means at no time, no matter how much you want to, never, ever, INTERRUPT them. As soon as you interrupt them, you will shut down the communication and they will interpret this as saying, "I am more interested in you hearing my side of the story than hearing yours."

I know that this goes against most people's natural tendencies. The key to resolving differences is to actually experience them, deal with them, and bring them to closure one time, not several times, not partially resolving them or half figuring them out. There is an old commercial that said, "You can pay me now or you can pay me later." Why not deal with the problem and pay now versus hoping to avoid the problem and pay (at a higher price) later.

Now that you have conveyed that you want your partner to continue, it is important to expand what they are willing to tell you. You want them to go deeper so that you can understand how much agreement there is between the two of you and what still needs to be compromised on, or discussed.

We do this by asking questions. Asking questions says, "Continue, and go this direction." This is important: do not minimize the power of asking someone questions. We do this by saying things like, "So help me understand this" or "Tell me where you are at with this." Asking questions invites them to continue and go deeper.

The last part of empathic listening is to literally, as empathy suggests, walk in the other person's shoes and try to understand things from their point of view. When we understand how someone else is experiencing something, we communicate that we understand him or her **up to that point**. This allows them to feel heard and to continue deeper.

The final stage of empathic listening is to paraphrase back to them what they were saying. We do this by saying things like, "So what you are saying is," or "You're disappointed because I did this." To the extent that we can add both the emotional component and the situation to the response, we strengthen our case that we truly understand what our partner is experiencing. An example might be, "So you're frustrated with me because I said I would not spend over $100.00 on clothes and I did" or "I know that I disappointed you when I went to those websites."

Be prepared: empathic listening may open lines of communication that have been left unexplored for many years. This means that there is potential for the floodgates of emotion to open and your spouse to vent the emotional backwaters of the dam. Your partner may tell you what they have wanted to tell you for several years but have been unable to. This is the time, as I tell my client's, "to be quiet and listen." Do this regardless of how uncomfortable it is to hear their pain and all the negative emotions they have built-up surrounding you. Do not shut this down and do not flee. This process is extremely therapeutic and cathartic; meaning it frees the emotions that have built-up simply by allowing them to be articulated.

How to Effectively Communicate Your Needs

The key to communicating your needs is to:

1. Say exactly what behavior your partner did, using specific language.
2. Tell them calmly how it made you feel. Share with them the emotional component. Tell them if you felt betrayed, frustrated, disappointed, etc.
3. Tell them the exact behavior that you would like them to do. No hinting, no generalization, no innuendos. Just tell them what you want the picture to look like.

Chapter Eleven

Wisdom on How to Get Along With Your Partner

1. Never Criticize Your Partner In Public or In Front Of Family or Friends

When we praise someone, especially when we do it in front of other people, it means a great deal to that person. Despite the fact that it is a little embarrassing, it matters twice as much. I see this type of behavior only in the happiest, most well adjusted couples. They are the first to say what a good cook their husband is or what a good tennis player their wife is. Always remember to praise in public and bring up shortcomings or things you would like them to work on *in private*. When we air our dirty laundry in front of people, especially those whom our partner wants approval from, we are really being hurtful.

Relationships are like houses. From the street, most houses look nice. The people in them must be perfect. The yard is mowed, the bushes are trimmed, and the house looks light and warm inside. However, most of us understand that once you get around the back of the house, you start to see what they are trying to hide. Once we get inside the house, we start to get an idea of how nurturing and healthy the family really is. Few houses are as they appear. The trouble with criticizing our partner in public is that this breaks down the image we are all trying to establish on how healthy and adjusted our house is. Sharing with people the intimate details of our mates or things that they are trying to hide is hurtful. This is usually a desperate attempt to get the person's attention and let them know how unhappy they are in the relationship or to hurt them. Either way, the response to this is to take off the gloves and try and hurt back.

Here is another reason not to criticize in public: what research suggests is that what we say about other people is not attributed to them. On the contrary; what we say about other people is attributed to *us*. If we were to say, "Beth is so sloppy, she will walk past something the kids have spilled, like cereal, and not clean it up." What people hear in this situation is that *you* are lazy and sloppy, not your wife. Likewise, if we hear someone say, "I am pretty lucky to have him. He is about the best dad I know." What people take from this situation is that *you* are a good parent. If you think about this honestly, you will probably agree.

2. Don't Put Them Down or Insult Them

Does insulting your partner work? Does wounding your partner with words get you what you want from them? Typically not. Hurting our partners is a strategy to manipulate by bullying them or to hurt them back for something we felt they hurt us over. It is generally seen as immature and desperate. Mature, well-adjusted couples don't use this strategy. Sometimes we have to be the one to lead. This means that by avoiding this strategy, we lose a tool that we have historically used to deal with an argument, but we look mature and increase the chances we will actually solve our problem. Remember, as soon as the gloves come off and our partner starts to insult us or put us down, nothing is going to be resolved.

3. When You See Your Mate Making Improvements, Tell Them

A lot of marital relations have been undone in the early stages of reconciling by one of the partners being unwilling to say (largely due to pride), "Hey, thanks for making a change." We need to be able to say, "I know it's not perfect, but I can tell you're trying and that means a lot." Many people ask for change, but then don't tell their partner or reinforce their partner when they do the very thing they have been asking them to do for years. Frequently, when I ask, "Why didn't you tell her that you appreciate her not spending so much money on groceries?" The answer I hear is, "Well, I was waiting for her to go back to her old ways," or "Well, it wasn't totally what I was fully asking for, I wanted her to spend less than $100.00 and she still spent $107.00." Initial changes are rarely what we want the picture to look like.

Change is made of successive approximations or *little changes* that are closer and closer to the way you want your partner to be. Reinforce these! Show your mate that you see a change. This does not mean they will stop there and never get to the way you really want them to be. Be patient, but give them something. This lets them know that you recognize their efforts and you appreciate them being aware of their behaviors. When people feel that they are being *changed*, they feel like they are giving up a part of their identity; they are getting away from the way that they were raised or the way that they are comfortable with doing something. People only change when they really want something. When you are asking people to change, however, you need to be willing to ignore some of their old behaviors. You need to make an effort to catch your partner being good. In other words, wait until you see the change that you want and then say something about recognizing this. This is a huge boost to the future of the behavior you want to see. Reinforcing any behavior increases the chances that it will occur again.

4. Don't Use Guilt Inductions

Guilt can be used as a device to prick our conscience or to make us feel remorseful for the things we have done wrong. It is used to make us feel bad about something. The problem with guilt inductions is that they work *in the short run*. In the long run, over time, they leave us feeling like a child that has misbehaved. We feel guilty for our behavior, but we get the sense that we are once again being parented. This is bound to cause resentment because no one wants his or her partner to take on the role of wife/parent or husband/parent. Few relationships can tolerate the relational dynamic evolving from lovers and equals to one of parent/child. It's not attractive and is inevitably going to cause resentment and frustration.

Not only do guilt inductions cause resentment due to changes in the sense of not being equals, but they also set up a perception that the one who is initiating the guilt induction is morally superior. This is why parents and the clergy use this strategy. The reality is that most people know what they did wrong; they don't need anyone dredging it up and shoving it in their face. It only reiterates that they have made a mistake. When you have the opportunity to dredge things up but don't, it sends a message of maturity and the sense that you want to work on the problem—not make someone feel like an immature 15-year-old.

When you come to the Y in the road and choose the path of trying to make your mate look immature, you may win in the short run. In the long run, they will be angry with you for your choice. However, when you have the opportunity to do this but choose instead to focus on the problem behavior and how it makes you feel, you are granted more respect because you had the chance to make them feel bad and you passed it up. Trust me, your partner knows when you could take an opportunity like this and make them feel worse about themselves. When you keep this information to yourself and don't share their behavior with the world, your credibility goes up and your partner's respect for you goes up. This gives you the chance to honestly work on the problem behavior. *If you do a guilt induction, you almost always lose your opportunity for resolving the problem.*

5. Be Patient

The line from where you are to where you want to be is not a straight line. How wonderful it would be if all we had to do was say, "Hey, can you start doing this different?" and it would start to happen immediately; your partner would never revert back to their old way of doing business. In a short period of time, they started doing things just the way you wanted them to.

There are days when you will see improvements and have hope. These are followed by days when your partner reverts back to their default mode or the way they came from the factory. This brings out our fears. Will they ever be the person you need them to be? If you were to chart the changes, there would be good days and bad day. There will be days of improvement, but there are bound to be days of reverting back to prior behaviors or only showing small gains. Sometimes they have a good day and do things exactly the way you wanted them to. This is followed by two or three days of almost no gains or inconsistency. You have to be patient. Don't give up too easily. These days are bound to be followed by days of improvement and change for the better. Don't expect perfection too quickly. This type of change takes time and is not necessarily going to change due to insight. Insight, or realizing something on a cognitive level, does not necessarily mean behavior change.

What you are looking for is what I call integration. For something to be integrated, it has to become part of the person's way of doing business. Not just a temporary change they will do under enough pressure or scrutiny. You want real change and that takes time.

In psychology 101, they teach you about reinforcement. Reinforcement says that if, following a behavior, you are given something that makes you feel good, the chances of you engaging in that behavior again increases. Reinforce the behavior that you want to increase. If you see the behavior that you want or close to the behavior you want, then say something or do something. A small hug at the appropriate time goes a long way toward saying, "I saw what you did, thank you."

However, I hear a lot of people say, "I don't expect my partner to tell me, 'hey thanks for cleaning the house or doing my laundry. Why should I have to say thanks to them?'" There are two problems here.

The first is the problem of changing behavior. The second is the issue of pride. Let me start with behavior change. Changing behavior that has been part of the way that a person has acted for years is difficult. It is not impossible, but difficult. A person has to become aware of their behavior and how it is affecting their partner. They may even have to realize that if they don't change, the relationship might end. Even then, as you know, this may not be enough to cause change. Reinforcing the changes you do see increases the probability that they will change.

Change is fighting an uphill battle. It was probably learned earlier in life, has been reinforced for some time, and it has a connection to a person's sense of identity, or how they see themselves. People hate to feel like they are the child and their partner is the parent making them change a behavior. When we are being asked to modify our attitudes or behavior, it may feel like we are the child and our partner is the parent who wants us to change. Nobody likes this dynamic. This is all the more reason that a small message about noticing the behavior being changed is important. If a person doesn't really want to change (and who does?) and if they can say to themselves, "Hey, I made the changes for two weeks and they never even noticed, why continue?" They won't. People don't like to change. If this behavior is important to your marriage, lose the battle but win the war. Lose the ego battle but win the behavior war.

This gets to the issue of one's pride or ego. Depending on how far into the relationship you are and how alienated you are from your spouse, this is either going to be difficult or *really difficult*.

As you start to grow distant from your partner, you start to decrease the amount of physical touch you give, the intimacy, the softness, and the looking into their eyes. The very reinforcement you used to give, and that they wanted, is lost. When you are distant from them emotionally, it is difficult for you to swallow your pride and be nice to them; especially since you haven't been nice to them in a while.

This is what I mean when I say lose the battle but win the war. The battle is for pride and the war is for happiness. By giving up your pride, being softer to them and reinforcing them for changes in their behavior, there is a risk. There is no guarantee that by reinforcing them they will change. There is very little chance that they will change if they don't see some reinforcement. It is a bit of a standoff, but somebody has to be the bigger person.

What I normally hear at this point is, "Well, I don't want to send a double message." We do want our messages to be consistent. What I tell my clients is, "You have been sending the same message for four years and it hasn't given you the improvement you want." This is usually just one more barrier in the issue of pride and ego. We don't want to be uncomfortable. We don't feel that it should be our responsibility to make our partner change or be the person they are supposed to be. Why should we have to be their parent?

Once again, this becomes a matter of how important the relationship is? What will you do in order to get the picture to be the way you want it? Pride can be a good thing, but it can also keep us from getting what we want in a relationship. Lose the battle of pride, but win the war of happiness.

Chapter Twelve

LEARNING YOUR BASICS

The basics are a set of *measurable behaviors* that start to be revealed after five or six sessions. After these sessions, the relationship is starting to improve. By that, I mean that there is more intimacy, more laughing, and teasing in the relationship. There is a sense of wanting to be with the other person, less walking on eggshells, feeling less awkward, and certainly more hope that the relationship will continue to improve. What is revealed are the things that both members are doing which are responsible for the relationship feeling better. I call these the Basics.

What are the basics? Basics are those things that, if we went back and graphed the level of closeness in the relationship, would have had the most impact. These basics are the behaviors that most contributed to this improvement. What things did the couple do for each other that could be seen, recognized, and appreciated? What made these differences? What I normally do is cultivate these and draw attention to them so that the couple can see that there is a change. Each realizes, *"I have made a change. I am doing something different."*

Frequently, men say things such as, "I am coming home earlier, I have thrown in a load of laundry, I am doing things the first time I am asked, or I am at least acknowledging that I heard what she asked me to do. Now I tell her when I will get around to doing something versus just letting it pass. I am golfing less, and I am spending more time with the kids." Those things were noted as his wife's "basics," the three or four things that she said were deal breakers and were causing a lot of resentment.

Women typically say, "I am not shopping as much as I was, and I am smiling at you more often. I am spending more time with you and less time with the kids. I am carving out time for us to be together. I have been aware of when I am bitching or asking you several times to do the same thing."

These things are often times very apparent to our partners, but not necessarily to us. These are often the little things that characterized the first and often happiest time of the relationship, but were lost or given up when the arguing started. Sometimes, these things were seen as tit for tat; meaning that as long as she is willing to do them, I will, but as soon as she quits doing them, so will I. It's almost like it is a hurtful game.

Understanding one's basics is important. They act as a template or model against which the couple must compare itself. It's the snapshot of the relationship, the picture of what was working in the relationship when things seemed good. Unless something new has happened in the relationship, the basics act as the list of things the couple needs to get back to in order to return to the prior level of intimacy and connectedness.

Our basics are the four or five things that the couple has to focus on to ensure that there are fewer arguments, more hope, and less resentment. Writing the basics down is a powerful step. I ask them to store this list in a special place (perhaps one's top drawer of their dresser). When things seem that they are deteriorating and the couple is feeling less connected, they need to pull out their list and see if they have kept their part of the bargain. Are they still doing the things that were on their list of basics? Did the situation change or did they get complacent? Did they get lazy? Do they need to get back to their therapist or back to their basics?

What I tell couples is this: If you graphed most relationships, you would see periods where the line went up and periods when the line went down. When the line went up, the relationship was better. What characterized this period? Almost invariably, the answer is, they were working on their basics. They were both doing what they knew they needed to do to keep things good between them. And then we look at the theoretical graph and ask why did the line drop? What was going on here? Once again, the answer is customarily, they quit doing things for each other, the kids came along, they started focusing on them, and there wasn't any time dedicated for date night. I also hear, "I started a new job." Or the classic, "We started to argue, and we weren't resolving our differences."

When couples find their BASICS, and work with them, they seem to be able to maintain the integrity of the relationship and thrive as a couple. However, what happens in at least a third of the relationships is that something happens and the couple reverts back to the old default way of doing business. During times of financial stress, work stress or some other strain on the relationship, they forget what was working (but took energy focus and resources). They reverted back to the dysfunctional way of interacting that got them into trouble earlier. The carving time out for date night, coming home early, helping with the chores, and spending time with the kids went by the wayside. They reverted back to some very basic, time honored ways of doing business. Maybe they got selfish and engaged in "scratching our itch" behaviors; the behaviors that help them through times of stress, the working, the golfing, the hunting, the spending; the work-in-the-short-run-but-not-in-the-long-run behaviors. They work almost as medicine to make them feel better. That is why they became behaviors they relied on to begin with, they work. However, as has been articulated, they have serious consequences when relied on too heavily or too often. They forgot the basics.

What Would Make You a Six?

The process of being in couple's therapy means that the couple starts to understand the things which are causing problems in the relationship. What is causing the resentments that are fueling the resentment dynamics? Sometimes, we have a very good idea of what our partner wants us to be or what they want us to do to make the relationship better. Our insight is good, we know what they want, but perhaps our pride, ego, or self-discipline keeps us from making the changes they want us to make. It keeps us from being the person they want us to be. Sometimes we have an idea in our minds about what we think our partner wants us to change, but that change is not even close to reality. It is only through asking what they *really* want us to do differently is the truth exposed.

One of the ways that I end almost every session is to ask, "On a scale of 1-10, what are you?" I ask them, "if '10' is soul mate, '5' is do I stay or do I go, and '1' is I could care less about my partner, I hope they find someone nice (total indifference), what are you?" Basically, I am trying to find out how alienated the clients are from each other. Are you a '5.5?' Someone who said they were a '5.5' is someone who is just on this side of staying. They are very close to the point where they say, if you ask me on any given day, I would either tell you I am staying or I am ready to leave. That is a '5'. A '10' is someone who is unbelievably happy in their relationship. These people don't usually enter into therapy. The caveat to this is that I do occasionally see couples where one of the individuals is happier than the other. Usually, however, if one of the people in the relationship is unhappy, the other is somewhere pretty close.

A '1' is someone who is absolutely indifferent to his or her partner. The opposite of love is not hate. Hate implies that you still care about someone. Indifference is the opposite of love. Ask anyone who has been divorced for a while, "Do you still hate your ex?" Chances are good they will say that they could care less about their ex. Ask anyone who is in a relationship and who is extremely alienated if they are angry with their mate. Chances are good they will say, "No, I don't care what happens to them. I hope they find someone nice and leave me alone."

Rating one's attachment to their mate is significant. This gives a couple a chance to think about how alienated they are from their mate or how close they are to them. Often times, there is little difference in the number. If one member says they are a '5', the other is usually not too far off. However, as I stated before, occasionally there is a man who is a '9', but whose wife is walking out the door emotionally and who is really unhappy at home.

Hearing our partner's rating can be painful for many people who have been unwilling to see the other's unhappiness or to leave the safety of denial. The first part of the question is what number are you? Sometimes, if the individual is having a hard time answering the question, I rephrase it to, "What is your range? Do you go between a four and a six? Between a six and a seven?"

The second part of the question is, "What would make you a ...?" (fill in the blank). Typically if their mate is a '5', I don't ask for too much of a stretch. "What would make you a '5.5'? What would your partner have to do (that is measurable) for three weeks that would make you a '5.5'?" The only exception that I take off the table as an option is sex. Sex can't be asked for as the thing that we want our partner to do to make us happier in the relationship.

What most people say is, "Since he doesn't usually come home until 8:00, I would be a '5.5' if he would come home every night before 6:00." Men sometimes state, "I would be a '5.5' if she would quit arguing with me," or "I would be a '6' if she would quit criticizing me."

The rating of one's relationship usually starts the discussion for the next session which is focused on the behaviors that the other wanted to be paid attention to. Did they respond to the thing that was said to make them a '6'? Were they better this week? My clients usually ask for the behavior that will provide the biggest bang for the buck. These are important because these are characteristically the Deal Breakers in a relationship. As a rule, these are noted as significant and usually end up being one of the three or four basics that, if applied on a regular basis, leads to less resentment, more closeness, and fewer arguments to begin with. As this process continues and the couple gets to the area of '8s'" or '9s', the behaviors that are asked for are normally seen as more polish than deal breakers.

These behavioral changes take time, they take awareness, and they take self-discipline. The person making the changes has to be willing to make the changes with the understanding that there are no guarantees that there will be any return on their investment. However, when one partner sees the other working on their issues, it makes them feel hope and slightly closer to their partner emotionally. Usually when we see a change in our partner's behavior, we tend to be prone to reciprocate and make some changes of our own.

Chapter Thirteen

THE MOST COMMON DYNAMICS THAT LEAD TO RESENTMENT

Resentment When We Don't Feel a Minimal Level of Connectedness

What is the minimal level of connectedness? When I am doing therapy with clients, I frequently meet with a couple together, but then also meet with each member of the couple individually. This is often to deal with issues that are specific to that client and not necessarily a topic for couples counseling such as one individual's anger management issues or substance abuse. Other times I meet with individuals separately because I want to meet with one of them in particular. I don't want to set up the dynamic of one of the individuals being the sick or most broken one. I want to avoid this. Sometimes my sense is that there is an issue that needs to be addressed that may be counter-therapeutic should it be broached when both are present. Issues such as other gay or lesbian relationships or infidelity are examples. Issues such as these, if broached in the couple's session, might damage what integrity the relationship still has so I frequently deal with them individually.

One of the things I frequently hear (primarily from women), is what I refer to as the minimal level of connectedness. The minimal level of connectedness is defined as *the least amount of interpersonal connectedness they can tolerate and still stay emotionally bonded with their mates.* Some women might measure this in terms of the number of hours spent together or the amount of time spent with their mate. Others may measure their minimal level of connectedness by the depth of conversation or sharing that goes on between them, regardless of the amount of time physically spent with their partner. Many women have their emotional batteries recharged by laughing and being teased by their husbands or by sharing a brief moment of connectedness with a few supportive words such as, "Don't worry, we will get through this". Some women feel closer as a couple when any of these are met.

No woman has the exact same criteria as another and only they know what it takes to make them feel connected. My experience is that most women know to almost the nth degree how much time or what it takes to make them feel connected or stay connected to their mates. Women need to feel emotionally connected in order to feel secure about their future, less anxious, and sexually receptive. My experience is that men also have this same need for connectedness, but perhaps not to the same degree as women.

This lack of emotional connectedness is for many women a deal breaker; in other words, a reason to exit the relationship. I rarely have men coming to me and stating that they are considering getting a divorce because they don't feel emotionally connected to their wives. Women will say that if they don't feel this minimal level of connectedness for a long enough period of time, they are losing the sense of connection with their husband and are considering a divorce. This can be seen as really two different things.

The first is the disconnection they feel from their mates and the other is the length of time they are experiencing it. Most women are able to tolerate this disconnection for a brief period of time; up to two years or so. Eventually, they start to feel detached or disengaged from their mates and this is unacceptable for them. This disconnection constitutes abandonment of the highest degree, even if their husband is there financially or physically. Most women say that this is not enough and they need physical affection and emotional connection in order to stay interested in maintaining the relationship. Without this need being met, they feel they have been abandoned.

Sometimes what happens is that early on in the relationship there was an emotional bond. When this deteriorates, it feels like a special type of betrayal because it says that given enough incentive, their husbands *were* capable of emotional intimacy. Women feel that now they are being taken for granted and that their partner simply isn't interested in putting as much energy into the relationship as he once did. This feels like a bait and switch because she feels she was lured into the relationship under the belief that emotional intimacy was something that would be maintained and would characterize the more mature long-term phase of the relationship.

Another situation is one where the woman is somewhat blinded by the initial attraction or chemical/infatuation phase of the relationship. After that phase has passed, they realize they have bonded with a man that is either not able to connect intimately with them or (more likely), is simply guessing at what she is talking about when she tells him what she needs or what is missing. In some cases, therapy will help this condition. I call it leaving a trail of bread crumbs. What I do is help husbands or boyfriends to understand what their mates are looking or longing for on an emotional or intimate level.

When an individual's minimal level of connectedness is not being met, they start to think about ending the relationship. When our needs are not being met, we start to look for *alternatives* to the relationship. Sometimes this means getting a divorce or leaving the primary relationship. Sometimes this means looking for an individual to have an affair or temporary relationship with. All of this follows the goal of getting their emotional needs met. Women most often have affairs to feel connected, men to feel sexually connected and desired.

Men also feel this need for emotional connectedness; some of the more sensitive ones as exquisitely as women do. It is only when they have this need for connectedness met that these men feel intimate, bonded, or close enough to feel interested in approaching or responding sexually to their mate.

The reason the issue of the minimal level of connectedness is important is that men often need to be left a trail of bread crumbs to help them understand some of these concepts. It is often said in psychological circles, "We value in others what we value in ourselves." In other words, if we value some trait in ourselves, such as the ability to feel and communicate emotions, then we believe this is an important trait in others. We value others more if they are able to feel and get in touch with their emotions. However, if we believe the showing of emotions only signifies weakness or a chink in somebody's armor, or sentimentality that can be taken advantage of by others, (as some more rational or logical people do), then we don't value it and in fact see it as a weakness or character flaw to be avoided. We don't appreciate it.

If men don't perceive this need for connectedness as existing because it doesn't exist in their world or they don't see the value of it, they would be missing out on understanding the single biggest factor to maintaining a long-term relationship. If men don't see the need to maintain emotional connectedness or if they are only guessing at how to establish it, they are being set up to fail in their goal of a long-term relationship. Sometimes, women themselves are aware of this need to stay connected to their mates, but have difficulty articulating it. They have a hard time finding the words, or (more often than not), communicating the actions or behaviors which make them feel connected.

What I often see is that men don't always understand such a need exists and more importantly how imperative this level of connectedness is. If they don't understand it exists, they may not understand what a woman is talking about when she says, "I don't feel connected to you." Likewise, women may not be able to articulate what their needs are or simply write this difference off to men in general. Women sometimes need help articulating what they mean by the minimal level of connectedness. Sometimes they make statements like, "I don't feel close to you." It is only when I help women articulate this to their husbands that men seem to understand. I understand that most women prefer that their husbands get their thoughts and their needs intuitively, but sometimes women need to leave a trail of bread crumbs for their mates about how they get their cup filled. This is how I feel connected to you. This is how I feel more sexually receptive to you. This is what you say to me or this is how you talk to me that makes me feel intimate with you. When you carve out time for me, when you would usually be spending it on something that is important to you and you give it to me, that is when I feel valued and prioritized. That is when I feel like I am first on your list, not when you just say that I am.

My observation is that many women have a test for their mates that goes like this: "If you intuitively sense my needs because you get me and we are so connected that you, without needing to ask, pickup my need for connectedness or how to connect with me, you and I are on the same wavelength and you love me."

I don't know if this is a recent phenomenon or if this has its roots in evolution. What I do know is that 70 percent of all men don't know that such a test exists or that they are being tested and are failing. Some men get this test and intuitively or naturally sense their mate's needs or what they need to say to get extra credit. Men can be coached to understand this need. Though they don't get the extra credit that some men get, the light bulb finally goes on and they at least get a B for effort.

Even if it does not come naturally, it counts for a lot. For many women this is the difference between feeling close enough emotionally and not enough feeling emotionally connected. Even glimpses of being emotionally connected makes a woman ask herself, "Will he eventually be able to give me the emotional cup filling that I need?" I can't say enough about how important this is to a woman.

Many women say that this is a deal breaker and the relationship without this is not good enough to stay in.

If I have learned one thing in twenty years of doing couples counseling, it is that the need to stay emotionally connected to your mate is HUGE. No other feature of a relationship better predicts the outcome than the ability to establish and maintain emotional connectedness. If a woman feels connected to a man emotionally at least once every two weeks, she can forgive almost anything.

Resentment When We Are Not Getting Enough Attention

When working with clients, I sometimes use the metaphor of baffles. Baffles are devices that are used to divert air within air ducts. We have a certain amount of energy that we are given each day. The average amount is arbitrary; for our discussion here we will call it ten units. Ten units of energy is usually enough to power our bodies for our pre-work grooming, an average workday, and just a little play. Most people get ten units–some a little more, some a little less. We can dip into another day's energy if we need to do something difficult. This is known as going to the well. We can do this, but not on a consistent basis without paying a heavy emotional and physical toll.

Out of us flows this energy and we baffle it or shunt it off to certain activities. We normally have the baffles wide open to things like our children; they routinely get a good deal of our energy. Some people put a lot of energy into their home and spend hours and several of their units of energy to keep it clean. All of the energy that flows out of us is diverted to one of several areas. The reality, however, is that the baffles are never set in stone. They are constantly being moved around and diverting different levels of energy to different activities. This means that sometimes our parents are having health problems and we need to spend a week with them until they are out of the hospital. Sometimes this means that our job is especially needy of our time and we need to spend 50 or 60 hours working for the next few weeks.

Managing our energy efficiently is what allows us to cope with all of the responsibilities we have to complete in a day. This is a fast paced and extremely technical age and most people feel that they do not have the job of one person, but rather they are doing the job of two or three people. It creates stress in our lives. Mankind's energy level has not kept up with his ability to cope with everything he has to do in an average day. We are frequently overwhelmed and feel we are stretched beyond what we have the energy to complete.

Because life is so difficult, most people have to make difficult decisions about how they use their precious energy. This means they have to make daily decisions about who is going to get their energy and who they are going to steal from or who they are going to have to put off and give energy to another day. Most people have a default mode where they normally direct their energy. But as everyone knows, life has a way of throwing us surprises that try our coping skills and stretch our capacity to keep up.

Because our energy is so precious and we have so little of it, we hate to waste it on people and activities that we don't feel we get something in return. When we are in a satisfying, monogamous, exclusive relationship, it is easy to divert energy to the activities that maintain this. In fact, the relationship itself recharges our batteries and gives us added energy because of the happiness and contentment that we feel when we are in a satisfying relationship. We are energized, able to concentrate, and focused because we are centered. When we are not feeling connected emotionally to our mates or feel resentful and disconnected, why would we be surprised when we no longer feel like we want to divert our energy to them?

One of the things that I hear time and time again is, "I don't feel like I am his/her #1 priority." Most people are even mature enough to say, "Hey, I know that they *should* put the kids over me, but I feel like I am fourth or fifth on their list; behind work, their friends, family, etc." Nobody wants to feel like they are low on their partner's list of priorities. In a healthy relationship, the mate is either one or two on their partner's list. Even healthy relationships can only tolerate a mate dropping to three or four for a brief period of time before resentment and anger starts to develop.

This is where voting with our time comes in. Voting with our time means that we put our energy (the visible manifestation of our energy) where our priorities are. Every adult knows that *their* parents had their priorities. They had their work, which took up a certain amount of their time, the house, and then had to divide their free time. Where we split our free time says volumes about what is important to us; what is one, two, or three on our priority list. Even at an early age, we looked at how many times our father pushed us on the swing versus our sister or our brother. How many times did our mother dote on our sister and not us? We were acutely aware of where we were on our parent's list of priorities. We knew even when we were young that you vote for what is important to you by how much time you devote to it. We vote with our time.

So, when we feel that we are not getting our partner's time or that they are refusing to carve time out for us, we start to feel resentment. This is perhaps the most common resentment dynamic. Essentially, we feel that if we are third or fourth on our partner's list of priorities, they have found other things that are more important to them.

Resentment When Women Think Men Don't Get Them

I was on a plane recently and there was a woman and a man, who was clearly her husband, in the seat in front of me. The woman spent at least twenty or thirty minutes talking about her boss and how he didn't appreciate her work, how they all make better money than she did, how she does the real work, and how they would be screwed if she were to leave. This is a fairly common complaint from most women, and from what I can tell, legitimately so. The guy who was with her never lifted his head once and the only statement he made to even acknowledge that he heard what she was saying was to mumble, "uh-huh," on two occasions.

Clearly, what this woman wanted to hear from her husband were words of support and acknowledgement for the validity of her situation. Herein lays the problem: one of the things that I have noticed about men is, that for many of them, they are just guessing about what a woman needs to hear when she is upset with something. The other thing that I have noticed is that men frequently do not have the emotional vocabulary to be able to communicate to women that they get them.

What I have learned is that not only do women need to know their significant other understands what they are going through, but women need to hear from their spouse things like, "It sounds like they don't appreciate you." This is all that most women need to hear to continue to even deeper levels of opening up and venting their frustration.

Women need to talk about what is irritating them; men not so much. This is one of the biggest ways that men and women differ. Early on in the relationship this is less of an issue, but as the relationship matures it is one of the things that typically changes. Ultimately, this ability to tap into what is bothering someone becomes one of the ways that women use to gauge whether her partner gets her or not; understands her or not. If her sense is that she has chosen a partner who doesn't get her, this starts a concern that she may have chosen the wrong guy and she starts to lose hope about their emotional future.

When I was a young graduate assistant in my doctoral program, I had the opportunity to teach counseling techniques.

One would think that for students of psychology and social work (most being natural students of human nature), learning how to connect to a client would be easy. Nothing could be further from the truth.

The problem is that most of the men in the program didn't have the emotional vocabulary to communicate to their clients that they understood what they were experiencing. We helped our clients to know we understand their pain by communicating back to them our understanding of the situation they were enduring. It made them feel we "got them." Sometimes this ability doesn't come so easily to men.

Women, on the other hand, seem to be much better as a group at communicating that they understand someone else's pain. This may be why they go to their friends to be understood. This isn't to say that some men are not good at it or can't learn to identify emotions and how to communicate that they get them, because they can. Women have to understand that men (even intelligent men), are frequently just guessing about what they are experiencing and how to give support through their pain and discomfort.

The other thing that women need to understand is that once in this situation, feeling like their husband doesn't get them, they may be vulnerable to being seduced emotionally by a man who is able to tap into their emotional pain. There may be a sense of, "Wow, finally a guy who gets me." This may be very attractive to a woman. A man who meets her needs emotionally may be appealing, but is he a good match for the rest of her needs? Is she better off leaving her husband and exploring relationships with other men who understand her emotional needs intuitively, but who do not have the degree of match, in interests, hobbies, parenting, religion, or other areas of her life?

Like water to a thirsty person, this need to be understood emotionally seems to trump our other needs; our need for having things in common for example. In the long run, however, women may realize that they would have been further ahead trying to help their mate understand the words they needed to hear, than by replacing him. Sometimes a woman is better off simply telling her husband that she doesn't want him to solve her problem, but to let her vent and share words of encouragement and support by saying, "Alright, I am listening."

Resentment When Our Need for Security is Not Met

People need security, they need to feel secure in their jobs, and they need to feel secure in their relationships. However, I don't believe that this need for security is always at a conscious level. I also believe that there is a continuum of security. On one end of the continuum is anxiety and on the other end is total security. What I have observed is that women seem to scan their environment to determine if their needs for security are being met. Women run through their list of things they need to be settled; the things they need to be resolved in order for them to lower their anxiety. When these needs are met, their anxiety quotient goes down and their security quotient goes up. It is difficult for things to be so unsettled as to cause anxiety. I see a teeter-totter effect for most women as they scan their environment and look at the indicators they use as a barometer of what constitutes security and whether those needs are being met.

This is not entirely a female phenomenon, but I see it much less frequently with males. For me, it is almost a part of being female. This experience is complicated and there are no hard-and-fast rules about what serves as a gauge of security.

What each woman needs to feel secure is as different as each female personality. There appears to be a number of common indicators, things that represent security so frequently that they are classic. What most women communicate is that they first look at, "Are the kids OK? Are the children healthy, are they warm, have they been fed, are they appropriately clothed? Are they physically and emotionally in a healthy place?"

Women appear to have an almost visceral "Ahhh" response to this so that when it is met, this increases their security and decreases their anxiety. Women now ask, "Are the bills paid? How are we doing financially and can we maintain the lifestyle that I want for my children and myself?" Once again, if the answer is yes, there is an increase in security and a decrease in anxiety. In essence, their anxiety level goes down and their security level goes up. "Does the house look nice? Would I be embarrassed to have my mother come over? Have the things that I wanted done by my partner been completed?" If she feels comfortable about her house, her anxiety, once again goes down and her security goes up. One of the areas that women differ from men is in this last category.

This is not to say that men don't experience the same thing as women, but they generally don't seem to experience it quite as exquisitely. This is the sense of, "Where am I at with my mate?" Women live in a world where they ask on a regular basis, "Am I emotionally connected, do I feel close to my husband? Have we been getting along, or have we been arguing?" When this is met, women experience a sigh of relief and their anxiety goes down and they experience security at a deeper level.

This sense of women thinking about how connected they are with their mates is huge and cannot be overstated. Due to this need for knowing where they are with their mates, however, they need data. They need information to feed into their internal computer to come up with a security quotient. The problem with this is that in order to get data, they have to be able to communicate with their mate. They have to be able to get past talking about the weather, the kids, and their jobs. They have to be able to talk about the real issues that give them trust and security, and help them to let down their guard. If a man can do this, if he can help her get to that place, the place of security, then he will experience the sense of her saying, "Ahhh, my anxiety went down and my security went up". She will experience a sense of peacefulness. This is a validation for women reading this book. Many will say, "Yes, that is exactly what happens. That is also why I bitch when my needs are not met."

(For men this is a road map. Because when you figure out how to give your mate this sense of security, you will be rewarded with a mate that is happier, less bitchy, and less likely to try and ask you a hundred questions trying to find the data they need to know where you are at emotionally with them).

Women say things like, "I feel really close to you this weekend." To which most men think, "What are you talking about? Yes, I guess we didn't' argue." This is where women live, yet men have no idea they have a stock that goes up and down depending on the degree that they connect with their mates, value them, and provide them with the security they seek. Women have developed to be motivated by security. For a large portion of them, this is where they live. They live in a world of security like men live in a world of sex.

The alternative to the previous dynamic where security levels go up and anxiety levels go down is that the opposite occurs and security levels go *down* and anxiety levels go *up*. When this dynamic occurs and life is such that between the bills, the kids, the house, and the marital relationship not being where she wants them to be, she feels apprehension, concern, worry and some fear. And because she is anxious and not comfortable with where her world is, *she is going to pass that on to her husband.* "I am going to let you know that I am not happy." For most women, this comes in the form of 'bitching', complaining, withholding sex, withdrawing, and (in some cases), becoming depressed.

As I stated before, my observation is that men are motivated by sex and women by security. This seems simple, but it is a complex issue. This book can't do the topic justice and even this brief discussion is only a simplified way of viewing them so we can discuss and put a framework around them. It is a very complex dynamic and I don't want to appear to make it too straightforward, because it is anything but. Clearly there are men that are more motivated by security than sex and there are women who are not motivated by either sex or security. It is a generalization that is only worthy of discussion because as a therapist I see it so often.

Resentment When Our Sexual Needs Are Not Met

If I had to pick one resentment dynamic that is most frequently communicated by men, it would be they are not getting enough sex and are therefore sexually frustrated. Often, sexual frustration is not the main reason that a couple enters therapy, but more often than not it is a core reason for their problems. There has been some other behavior such as an affair that has precipitated a breakup or a filing for divorce. This is the most common complaint for the men that I see, but it is also a complaint for women. Men do not have a monopoly on the need for more sex.

When there is infrequent sexual activity in a relationship, there is bound to be built-up sexual tension. This means that at an emotional or internal level, the individual is easily frustrated, easily agitated, and as I say "half way to pissed off" all of the time; this tendency to be edgy or tense leads to the downward spiral, because it increases two types of behavior; each initiating a resentment dynamic for different reasons.

The first dynamic begins, due to frustration and agitation, with a series of curt responses, decreases in eye contact, and a general sense of one's partner being upset or angry. This leads to a cycle of wanting to be with the person less–not more. As the length of time between sex increases, so does the level of agitation. The partner who is in need of release starts to engage in a series of inflammatory thoughts or thoughts that inflame or make them more angry. These thoughts range from, "They enjoy controlling me" to "They don't' love me. If they really loved me they would take care of my needs," or "Where are they having sex?"

When these inflammatory thoughts continue, they lead to less and less intimacy and a decreased sense of wanting to connect emotionally. This eventually ends up fueling itself and becomes a negative feedback loop. Men feeling sexually ignored, easily frustrated, pouting. This leads to women wanting to spend less time with them—not more. Plus, what is sexier than an agitated or pouting man? Hence, the woman does not approach him in an intimate way. The majority of people are only guessing at how to stop this dynamic and give their partner the connection they need. Hence, the dynamic continues frequently to the point of the person irrationally telling themselves that they are technically within their rights to have an affair or seek sex elsewhere, since their partner is unwilling to satisfy this part of the marital agreement.

The second dynamic involves the person who feels sexually neglected; becoming needy or more intimate and kind, almost disgustingly so. Almost every time their partner is around, they are touching, groping, and willing to do whatever their partner hints; as long as they will get the release they want. Almost like a lost and needy puppy, they are too attentive. This leads to a resentment dynamic of a different kind. In this dynamic, there starts to develop a sense for the woman of, "The only reason you want me is for sex." This starts a cascade of behaviors and attitudes which suggests that everything else the person does is not valued or appreciated. What I hear is, "The only time they give me attention is when they want something." This causes a withdrawal of feelings and not an increase in affection.

What I see fairly frequently is that the man in the relationship is a little naïve about how to give his partner the attention, emotional connection, or help that she needs in the relationship. This often leaves her resentful, feeling like she is unimportant, or a low priority in his life. Not only do women usually feel they are not a priority, but they feel overwhelmed and tired at the end of the day. This leaves them less interested in meeting their partner's sexual needs.

Women need to feel emotionally connected in order to have something as intense and personal as physical intimacy. Men don't need this level of connectedness; thus they don't realize that women need it. Due to this, they are entering into their relationship thinking like a man and not like a woman. The result is that they work too much, focus too much on their golf, hunting, or some other interest and then wonder why their partner is less than responsive at night.

These changes lead to the classic men's resentment dynamic where they complain that they feel they entered into a relationship with their spouse under the assumption that the way the relationship started would be the way the relationship remained. This means they thought that the woman they were dating would remain that way for the rest of their lives. They complain that she used to be happy, sexually receptive, and quick to laugh. She was easy going and not critical. In essence, it was easy to be with her. Then the realities of children, financial stresses, and job responsibilities materialized. A critical mass of resentment finally built-up enough to shutdown the very intimacy that was required for sexual activity.

Not only do their life stressors change, but the neurotransmitters responsible for infatuation and the early feelings of being in love also wear out. As I stated earlier in the book, they are replaced by other chemicals, with decidedly different properties. These brain chemicals still elicit a good feeling, but not the "wow" that the fall-in-love chemicals do. This means that men have to deal with the day-to-day responsibilities of early life stressors; i.e., never having enough money, being at the beginning of their career, and children. But they don't get to deal with them with the same level of feel-good brain chemicals. They don't get to go through them high on their wives.

Adding children to the equation is a huge change for men. Not because men don't want children, but they usually have no true concept of how much children are going to change their lives. With children in the picture, men are going to have fewer resources, less of the pie (meaning the amount of time left at the end of the day with their wife), and are usually going to get less sex. After taking care of most of the responsibilities of the home and childcare, women are usually exhausted at the end of the day and the last thing they report being interested in is, you guessed it, sex. So now the one thing that most men report drawing them into a relationship has changed, they feel that they were fooled and were the victim of a cruel bait and switch. Hence, they are resentful.

Resentment When Our Partner's Change

The thing about living longer as a society is that we have greater time to become something. I am not sure if this is the case in societies where the life span is shorter or where the predominant culture does not allow it. In the U.S. where we have the resources that allow a person to self-actualize, some people (if not most), are in the process of "becoming" something.

What is becoming? Becoming means that we are in transition from the person we were when we were young to the person that we are realizing that we want to be. This means that we move from what I quite often refer to as the way we came from the factory to the more polished version of *what we want to be.* Becoming something is a good thing, unless it takes you on a path that is in your best interest, but perhaps not your partner's. If you married in your early twenties before you had an identity (or it was a version of what your parents, husband, or culture wanted you to be), this may be difficult. Individuals in their second marriage often have less of an issue with this because they have already started the process of becoming what they are going to be. The problem with becoming is that it frequently takes on a passion of its own that then fuels it.

Examples of becoming might be the person's need to be a more educated person or a more spiritual person. Other examples might be individuals who want to lose weight or get in better shape. These are frequently things that people are extremely passionate about, and due to this, they serve to drive a person. Often these paths take a person in a different direction than their mate. This is particularly difficult when their mate is the exact same person they married. Resentment and frustration grows when we ask ourselves, "How can I respect them when they are the same person they were twenty years ago? They have no drive or ambition."

Sometimes our growth takes us on a journey with new friends or in a direction where our mates have no interest in going. Our becoming takes us down roads or in directions that are new for us, but not necessarily of interest to our mate. When we are excited about our growth, we naturally focus our time and resources on it. This frequently means there will be changes in where we spend our free time. This may mean college, out-of-doors, at church, or in the gym. If our mates are not as passionate about these places, this may cause problems. There is an old saying, "Where your heart is, so is your mind." Our thoughts, what we are thinking about, are usually on issues related to the world surrounding what we are becoming. It now becomes what we want to talk about all the time. This is a huge change.

We oftentimes become obsessed with our new pursuits and interests. It is all we think about and what we want to share with our mates. However, if they are not interested or perhaps see these things as a threat, they may be less than happy to engage in these discussions. This means that the communication decreases and the resentment increases. Occasionally, there is enough honesty on the part of our mates to admit, "I am afraid you are going to outgrow me." There are natural fears that if the person they married has matured spiritually, they will not be happy with someone who does not have a religious life. Sometimes people have fears their mate will become too educated and outgrow them in terms of their career and this will lead to them being left behind as their partner meets different people in their new job. For many of those left behind, there is nothing to talk about.

What is the answer when one member of a pair has the urge to grow beyond what the other mate is comfortable with? Can relationships survive this type of personal growth? The answer is absolutely YES!

The key is to be able to discuss the issue of the newfound passion without becoming defensive and argumentative. This growth does not have to be a threat to the core relationship. How can the remaining member of the pair gain security? Does there need to be discussions about the pace of growth; can one take classes gradually or must they work on their degree full time? Must all weekends be focused on the pursuit of their passion or does there need to be time partitioned out or carved out for the family and the remaining member of the couple? If resources are a problem, can there be a frank discussion about where the money will come from to pursue one's growth?

When we don't feel short-changed with the time that we need and are given assurances that this does not mean the end of the relationship, this increases the chances that what the person's partner is focused on will be less intimidating. Most people want their husband and wife to be happy. When we look for the win-win in this situation, there needs to be acceptable levels or timelines for when you will get where you want to be, how much time will be spent on getting there, how much of our resources will be spent on getting there, and "What you will you do with me once you get there?" Only when these questions have been answered will there be peace in the family and less resentment felt by the partner who feels they are being left behind.

Resentment Over Bitching Or Nagging

One of the most common sources of resentment for men is the feeling that they can't do anything right and their wife is bitching at them all the time. I think if I were to break it down, I would say that there are two basic reasons that women nag or complain.

My general feeling is that 75 percent of the time the reason is that the woman is not feeling heard. Let's say that a woman wants the garage cleaned. They might say something like, "That garage is a mess." Typically, the man says, "Ah huh," but does not look up from the paper he is reading. Usually the woman doesn't feel she was heard so, what does she say? In a different voice, "Boy it would be nice if that garage was clean" or "I wish I could get my car in the garage." When a woman doesn't feel heard she often feels like she must come at it from a different direction. The first direction didn't work. So, in a different tone of voice she tries communicating the same message. Eventually, she says in ever-increasing levels of agitation or sarcasm, "When are you going to clean the garage?" Oftentimes, I find that the man heard the woman the very first time she said she wanted something done, but for reasons of not wanting to appear henpecked, controlled, or having to jump when she calls, he does not respond as quickly as she would like. What most men say is, *"I heard her the first time she said something."*

As women get more and more frustrated because they don't feel heard or that their needs were understood, this raises a woman's level of anxiety. As a woman's level of anxiety goes up, this tends to ratchet up her voice and general level of agitation. She starts to have fears (whether it is the basement being painted or the garage cleaned), that it is never going to get done.

What I tend to see is that as the wife gets more and more frustrated, the better the chance she will engage in more desperate attempts to get his attention and hopefully develop a plan. She needs a plan so that she can have hope that her world will look the way she wants it to. What men say is that it gets more and more disrespectful; feeling like they are being talked to like they were a child. Ultimately, it ends up with more and more sarcastic statements. For example, "I guess that garage is going to have to clean itself." Or, "I guess if I want that garage cleaned I will have to do it myself." They end up in more and more disrespectful tones, which ultimately tap into a concern by men that they will be parented by their wives. They feel they've become the 14-year-old adolescent son who doesn't want to do some chore and their wife is their 40-year-old mother.

This is a dynamic that is frequently revealed in therapy. This perception on a woman's part is that she now has "another kid" and that she has been cast in the uncomfortable position of having to parent him. Because he is not taking responsibility for himself and what she believes he needs to do around the house or what he agrees to do, she feels she has to prompt him, bitch, or order him around like he was a teenager. The same issue is communicated from many of my men, who report that they feel that their wives now act more like a mother to them than an equal. Neither likes this situation, yet they are unclear on how to reverse this trend.

This is one of the times where both parties have to work on hearing the other person and communicate that they understood the message the other person was trying to send. If we don't communicate that we heard what our mates want done, they are forced to go to greater and greater lengths to get our attention or to get us to do what it is that's making them anxious. They feel that they have no choice but to come at it from some other direction or in some other way; some greater level which becomes louder or more agitated and only worsens the problem in terms of feeling disrespectful or feeling controlled.

I take a two-pronged approach to this problem. Men have to go further to communicate that they heard their wife's message. They also have to take more responsibility for doing what they said they would do. Men also need to be willing to negotiate (rather than ignore) when they will be willing (or under what circumstances), to perform the behavior they are being asked to do.

Women need to understand that they are getting into a cycle of increased levels of agitation, sarcasm, and perhaps disrespect. This type of communication style sabotages trust and respect in a relationship. This can lead to building up resentment; especially if women are in a relationship with a man who is not good at negotiating, communicating, or one who is not particularly motivated. Hence, we end up in a cycle of bitching or griping. This is one of the easiest resentment dynamics to resolve.

The second biggest reason that women bitch or complain is that they are feeling anxiety. Remember that women are generally motivated by security and when their security quotient is not being met, they often feel the need to share it with their husband. This can take on an air of bitchiness and accounts for roughly 25 percent of all bitching. The worst cause of irritability, and hence nagging, is the, "I am not happy and you are not going to be either," rationale. Though this type only accounts for a small portion of all irritability and complaining, it is by far the most disruptive and corrosive to the relationship.

Resentment Over Our Partners Being Untruthful

One phenomenon I see on a regular basis is my clients complaining of their mate's lying to them. I don't know how many times I have heard, "I care about them, but I can't trust them". What people worry about the most is, "Is this compulsive lying or situational lying?" The answer to this question is

"Depends." Most of the individuals that struggle with lying are doing so for one simple reason: escape/avoidance. It is easier to tell their partners something that will let them avoid consequences than to be honest and take their 'medicine.' Oftentimes, the problem is the medicine itself.

If the consequences are fair, most people will take them. Let's say on a scale of 1 to 10, the behavior that the individual engaged in would be considered a 3. This means that the time should match the crime. Thus the guilt induction, harsh words, incrimination, and general tongue lashing should match the gravity of the behavior triggering this incident. However, if the reaction to a 3 is a 9 or the perception is they will get pretty beat-up emotionally; many people will opt for taking their chances on not being discovered and try to avoid it by lying.

What I focus on for these couples is for the individual struggling with lying to focus on being aware of being tempted to lie and how this is going to affect the healing process. As I stated earlier, love and lying don't go together. What I also focus on is bringing attention to their partner's awareness of how harshly they are coming down on their partner and if this is fair. We also need to be able to say things like, "Thank you for telling the truth," when we feel that our partner has come to the Y in the road and taken the path that leads to honesty and taking responsibility rather than avoiding the consequences.

What I also work on for these individuals is the period before they are cast in a position of having to decide to tell a lie or take responsibility. If, for example, they actually did get the oil changed in their wife's car when they said they would, they don't have to lie about it when she asks. Eventually, women will look up at the little sticker and see if it has really been changed. Likewise, if women state that they will only spend $100.00 on clothes for the kids, they need to abide by their agreement.

This is because eventually their partner will see what is hidden in the closet or the trunk of the car.

People need to work harder on being organized and doing what they say they will do. Or, not say they will do something if they really can't (the knight in shining armor syndrome). They get credit for saying they will do something and make their wives or husbands happy. These can consist of things they either have some plan on actually doing or just receiving the credit for something, but have no plan on actually completing the task. We can't lie and remain in a happy marriage. If the lying is due to trying to escape and avoid something, either try to work on understanding the getting caught/consequence phase and learn to not over-react, or take responsibility for the thing you said you would do in the first place and just do it.

Resentment Over Clutter and Level of Cleanliness

In regards to issues around the home, an individual's threshold for what makes them anxious about the inside of the home often varies from person to person. By this, I mean the cleanliness of the home, the level of clutter, and the number of dishes in the sink. It is not uncommon for there to be a difference between a woman's tolerance for clutter and cleanliness and a man's. This is not always true, but it is common enough that I can mention it here.

Most women would like to see the house maintained at a certain level of cleanliness and men are comfortable with about two notches of clutter and cleanliness below that. I mean how much hair in the sink, dust, kids toys, and dishes in the sink, they are willing to tolerate. The issue isn't whether it is the man who is more interested in keeping the house clean or the woman.

The point is that if one person's threshold is different than the others, what is going to happen? Obviously, when one person's threshold is triggered, their anxiety is triggered as well. For them, there is a sense of, "This is too messy, this is too dirty, this is too dusty, what would happen if my mother came over and saw this? She would think I am not a good housekeeper." Their anxiety causes them to act. They feel the need to clean up the dust, clutter, or toys. So, what happens is there develops a resentment dynamic or cycle of resentment since their anxiety is higher than their partner's. In the end, they are frustrated and resentful because they are the ones doing the bulk of the cleaning and organizing. They were hoping there would be more equity in the workload. They are the ones engaging the behavior that they were hoping their partner (or perhaps both of them) would do. And so they are frustrated and resentful because they have to do all the work.

It is important to note that whoever has the higher tolerance for clutter and lack of cleanliness is not made anxious by the state of the house. Often they are not bothered by the messiness at all, and so they are not at all put out. They may even say, "If that bothers you, that is your business." In fact, their partner's cleaning may come as a welcome relief. What they don't realize that while this strategy works in the short run, it does not work in the long run. In the end, this is sabotaging the intimacy in the relationship because they don't see it as a problem. A wise spouse will say, "This really bothers me. I know that you don't care as much as I do about beds not being made, dishes in the sink, etc., but per our agreement and what we negotiated, you said you would clean this up or do this despite the fact that it does not make you uncomfortable."

People need to understand that just because their partner's anxiety gets triggered before theirs does and are compelled to clean up, this is not an excuse to not take their share of the chores. People know when they are being taken advantage of, being taken advantage of leads to resentment.

Arguing About Chores

One of the things I find about chores is that they are responsibilities that are negotiated or agreed upon. But as everyone knows, they are activities we are not particularly happy about engaging in. We all live in homes and homes have upkeep and responsibilities.

In the classic 50s model, the man took responsibility for the outside tasks; lawn maintenance, snow removal, and car maintenance. The woman took responsibility for tasks such as childcare, meal preparation, cleaning, groceries, and laundry. In today's marriage, each of these tasks is **negotiated**. Unlike the 50s model, in a modern relationship everything goes on the auction block and needs to be partitioned out or given to one of the parties (or agreed to be shared). What this means is that there is a premium on ones abilities to negotiate. Not only is there a premium on a person's ability to bargain for what they will and won't take as responsibilities, but also on the maturity it takes to actually do what they agreed to do! If you are in a relationship with someone who is good at negotiating and is also mature enough to complete the responsibilities they agreed on, count yourself lucky. The reality is you probably wouldn't be reading this book if you have this kind of relationship.

Many relationships are made up of people who are not good at negotiating or people who are unwilling to do things that they don't like to do, (even though they agreed to do them which gets to even deeper issues such as maturity and character). If you are in a situation where you used to be willing to do things that you didn't want to do but because you were getting sex, connection, resources or happiness, you did them, but now you are not, this causes a problem in a relationship. Particularly when the relationship is starting to deteriorate, this can cause a good deal of resentment.

This gets to the issue of the other persons level of anxiety. Things get left undone and leave people in a position of having to leverage things and continually prompt or bitch to get them completed. As stated before, this taps into that adolescent concern that they are going to be parented by their husband or wife. One of the examples I frequently share with couples is the issue of the garbage.

If I have agreed to take out the garbage in the kitchen and that is my responsibility and my wife says to me, "Can you take out the garbage?" and I get up and take out the garbage, then I get 100 points. We can call them credibility points or maturity points. I am agreeing to do what she asked me to do and this makes me appear mature and responsible. However, if I am watching TV or reading the paper and I my wife prompts me, "Hey, can you take out the garbage?" and I say, "Yes, as soon as I am done with this section of the paper or as soon as this show is over," then she has to repeat it or prompt me again. She gets a bit agitated and frustrated, but ultimately I complete it. When this is the case, I get 50 maturity points. If she goes through this process several times, however, she finally takes the bag out of the bin and starts to tie it up. I get up in a huff; I grab the bag out of the bin, and take it out to the herbie curbie. I do what she asks me to do, but how many maturity points, how many credibility points do I get? I get ZERO points for doing it. And yet, I did it! So, I did what it was she wanted me to do but she is still resentful. Subsequently, there are extra points involved in some activities. If I understand that it is my responsibility to take out the garbage, it is something I have negotiated to do as part of my upkeep of the house. If I go by the bin and realize that the garbage is particularly smelly and overflowing, so I bag it up and take it out. She comes and notices that the garbage, *that she was going to prompt me to take out,* has already been taken out. I don't require any prompting, nagging, or parenting. Then I get 200 maturity points. I have abided by my agreement and appear to be a grown adult; rather than an adolescent that needs to be prompted throughout the day to complete my chores.

Resentment Over How We Hand our Partner's a Message

Often, it is not **what** a person wants their partner do that causes a problem; rather **it is the way the message is handed to them that causes a problem.** Often if the relationship is strained, the way the message is communicated is rather blunt, without any degree of softening. Therefore, it is handed to them in a direct way, i.e., "You need to ..." People tend to respond to this negatively. It tends to bring up issues of feeling like they are being parented. One has to be sensitive when asking one's mate to do some type of chore or activity. Is the message that you are handing to your spouse palatable or easy to accept? Is their perception that your request is being handed to them in a way that they feel is heavy handed or disrespectful?

Sometimes the way we ask our spouse to do things around the house needs to be polished so that we get what we want and they get the feeling of being treated like an adult. I often ask individuals', "How do you want your spouse to ask you what they want you to do? How do you want them to deliver the messages regarding issues, chores, or responsibilities that you have negotiated, that you acknowledge are your duties? How do you want them to hand them to you?" Quite often, people say, "I want them to hand them to me in a more respectful way." This is easier in the early stages of a relationship, when there is less resentment and more passion and intimacy. But this can be particularly difficult when the relationship has suffered several years of damage. To now ask one's spouse to do something in a kind, respectful voice can get caught in a person's craw. They don't want to have to ask them in the first place; let alone have to do it in a nice tone of voice. Men, often state "I am a manager at work, I am a respected member of my community, I am a coach at little league, and I don't want to be talked to like a 14-year-old." Sometimes men say, "I would prefer she put it on a list. That bypasses any issues of how it is handed to me. Simply put it on a white board or dry erase board. Put the most important thing at the top of the list, so I know what the most pressing thing is to you. The second most important thing goes under that. Then I don't worry about how things are handed to me and I can focus on the message rather than whether I am going to passive aggressively not do it, put it off, or simply forget it. I will simply do it. Better yet, let's agree on a timeline so I can feel empowered and I can enjoy what I am doing and not feel that I need to jump right up and do your bidding. I can finish watching the game and know I have until 5:00 to finish my chores."

Resentment When Our Partner's Focus Too Much Attention on the Children

When people don't feel connected to their partner's, they typically tend to focus on their children or their homes. This may mean doting on their children and ensuring they are healthy and engaging in a variety of activities that will make them happy. It takes a good deal of time to get children back and forth to practices and recitals, so who can be faulted if a woman focuses on her children? This frequently precipitates a feeling by their husband, however, that he is second or third on her list. These men are feeling left out; citing their children, the house, or her career as being more important to her than he is.

Unfortunately, this circumstance does not bring an individual closer to their mate. The problem is that these activities work in the short run, but not in the long run. In the short run, they act as medicine to make a person feel better about themselves (connected to someone), so it is reinforcing in that way. However, they sabotage us because in the long run they act to pull us farther apart from our mates. Not only are we focusing all our energy and resources on these activities, but now our partners feel left out and like they are third or fourth on our list. We have gone on without them. Most men believed that they would be at least second on their wife's list of priorities and to find themselves third or fourth is extremely difficult. This often leads to feelings of being taken advantage of or being involved in a "bait and switch," when in fact this is not the case.

At this point, couples frequently ask themselves, "Is there anything here worth saving? Should we take the risks and try and work this relationship out or should we continue on this tangent and get our satisfaction, as we have for the last two years, through our other activities? Should I fan the flame of our love or should I put my energy into something where I will get a return on my investment? Aren't I just opening myself up to further failure and rejection? Will I put a bunch of time, energy, and hope into this relationship only to be disappointed, discouraged, and frustrated?" They ask these questions, because they have tried every home baked strategy in their arsenal to try and improve their relations and have failed so far.

Issues of Dominance

(Otherwise Known as Resentment about Who's Wearing The Pants)

What are issues of dominance? Issues of dominance refer to the role that each person plays in the leadership and decision making of a relationship. Dominance occurs across a continuum, from passive and dependent at one end of the scale to assertive and extremely independent at the other. It is important to understand that very few people find themselves at either end of the spectrum. If we looked at all the people in the world, they would tend to form a bell curve or normal distribution of people with very few people at the tails of the curve.

Like most bell curves, there are a lot of people in the middle. The rest of the population begins to occur outside of the middle and is in one of the two tails of the distribution. As with many distributions, to manifest in one of the two tails tends to make us more obvious and our characteristics more apparent.

Let's look at the passive end of the spectrum first. Very few people are extremely passive. Everyone knows someone who is so meek and submissive that they don't trust their own judgment and look to others to both complete them and to guide their decisions. When we encounter these people in therapy, we tend to diagnose them as passive-dependent personalities. Extremely passive people carry themselves in a way that cries out that they lack confidence. They send out a vibe which suggests they would be easy to manipulate or victimize. These souls are not at all self-assured or self-confident, and it shows in the way that they present themselves. Passive individuals look to be parented by another more competent and motivated person. This more dominant role is a role that they hate, and it scares them to think of being cast into such a powerful or influential role.

At the other end of the scale is the assertive, independent individual. Independent individuals are those who are more comfortable with the notion of taking charge of a situation or relationship and who actively position themselves to make decisions and wear the pants.

Moderately independent individuals quite often date other moderately independent individuals. Those that are moderately independent and well-adjusted are comfortable with other similar, self-sufficient individuals. What I tend to see are problems with individuals who find themselves at either end of the spectrum. I rarely see independent, assertive, take charge individuals dating or mating with another super-assertive individual. It is not that they don't find them attractive, because sometimes they do. The problem is that whenever you place two super-assertive individuals together, there are problems.

Let me give you an example: Two assertive individuals might have problems with simple decisions like, "What sounds good for diner, Outback or Chili's?" or with decisions as significant to the relationship as, "Where do we live, closer to your family or mine? How many children should we have?" or "Where do we spend our vacations, on the beach or in the mountains?" Whenever we have such significant issues to discuss and resolve, there is a good chance that resentment will be developed if both individuals in a marriage want to be the dominant one, the one to make the final decision. Likewise, when there are two passive individuals in a relationship, it can be difficult to make a decision as well (i.e., "Where do you want to go for dinner? I don't know where do you want to go?"). Extremely dominant individuals tend to gravitate to individuals that are more passive. More passive individuals tend to gravitate to more dominant or independent people. Both actually seem to like the arrangement. The super-passive individual doesn't have to make decisions and the super-assertive individual doesn't have to worry about not wearing the pants. It is a match made in heaven. Or is it?

The reason that issues of dominance are so important is that they are one of the biggest reasons that resentments build up and relationships don't work out. One of the problems is that once dominance is established, it is difficult (but not impossible) to change. Dominance is usually established early on in the relationship and may legitimately be the way that both people want to function within the relationship. This means that early on, one person may be the more dominant one, and the other easier going or more passive. Usually this person is comfortable or satisfied taking the role of the more passive member of the couple. This may simply be an early (and artificial) phase that the couple goes through on the way to a more evolved phase of the relationship.

Women often come by their confidence and sense of who they are later than men. Due to this, women frequently mature into their roles slightly later in life. Men often have an artificially immature version of what they want the relationship to look like based on the courtship, and they want this to continue. Therefore, they are surprised and resentful when their attempts to maintain the relationship at its freshman-like level are met with failure. Sometimes later into the couple's 20s and 30s, dominance is reestablished; based not on how it started, but on reality.

More often than not, a couple follows the traditional model of the man being the leader in the initial stages of the relationship. Then things change when he is unable to continue to increase his level of responsibility and continues to function as an eighteen or twenty year old. As he starts to be less and less of the adult that she needs, less and less responsible, the woman is cast in a position of becoming more and more the leader, the parent, and the dominant person in the relationship. This leads to resentment because the woman does not see herself as wanting to be in a more dominant role, but rather feels cast into a role that she is uncomfortable with; that of having to wear the pants or be the decision maker, the motivator, and the prompter in the relationship.

Not all relationships with a dominant person and a more passive person are doomed to failure. In actuality, I rarely address this issue because usually there is an understanding (perhaps on at least in an unconscious level), that this arrangement is working for the couple. For example, in many relationships I see a man who is satisfied in playing the part of the more submissive partner and who simply goes along with most of the decisions that his wife makes. The problem I see is that there is inherently a good deal of resentment on the part of the more dominant person in these relationships based on the sense that they, "have to make all the decisions." There is also a sense on the part of the dominant individual that while they love their partner, they have lost respect for them due to perceiving them as being, "weaker and more timid." As stated earlier, the two pillars that love stands on are trust and respect. How can the stronger person trust and respect their mate if they are so passive and tentative? Their resentment is also based on the psychological principle that we value in others what we value in ourselves.

Resentment bubbles up in the unconscious of the more passive individual as well. Many times, there is contempt for the stronger individual due to the sense that, "They have their hands on the steering wheel and their foot on the gas. I am only along for the ride. I have no control." It is not impossible for such arrangements to work successfully, but finding the right mixture of control and submission can be difficult.

Resentment Toward A Partner That Is Selfish

Rarely is it possible to have marital happiness without two people who both have a self-sacrificing attitude. By putting the needs of our spouse ahead of our own needs, we set up a dynamic of expressing our love in a tangible way; a way that can be seen. No one personality characteristic more predicts the fate of a marriage than the level of selfishness of the two individuals involved. Everyone knows of relationships where one person puts their own interests ahead of everyone else's. This is toxic to the relationship and sets up a dynamic where one person is selfish and taking care of their own needs first.

The sense that our mate is doing what is in their own best interest, rather than doing what is in the best interest of the relationship, affects a person's level of trust. By doing what is in our partner's best interest, we take a risk. If our mate is selfish, then we are the giver and they are the taker. We all know of such relationships. Resentment is never far behind.

Wise and mature people also take a risk by doing what is in their partner's best interest with the hope that they will return the favor and do what is in our best interest. This can create a positive cycle where we are each doing what is in the other's best interest. Just as a resentment dynamic is a negative feedback helix, cycling ever downward; an intimacy dynamic is a positive helix leading upwards to greater and greater levels of happiness and satisfaction. This also tends to increase the depth of feeling in the relationship. It means taking the attitude, "I'll put my husband's/wife's interests ahead of mine and hopefully he/she appreciates it and is willing to do the same for me." Now, all people have a portion of their personalities that are both selfish and selfless. Both are self-serving as well as concerned about the best interest of others; givers and takers.

The issue isn't whether we have these characteristics or not. The issue is the proportion of one set of qualities to the other. In other words, it isn't "Can my partner be selfish?"; but rather "How often are they selfish and how often do they do what is in my best interest?" Everyone has a proportion in their minds about what they need in a partner. My own equation is that my mate had better do what is in my best interest at least 85 percent of the time or I will feel that they are being selfish. If 15 percent of the time they are engaging in self-care or taking care of themselves by doing what they want for themselves, I harbor *no* resentment. In fact, couples **need** to carve out the time and resources to take care of their own needs, to recharge their own batteries.

When, however, the amount of time carved out exceeds that of the mate, when one is selfless and puts 99 percent (an almost perfectionistic level) of their time into the children and home while the other doesn't, there may be disappointment in their mate for being selfish. (Even though they may only engage in self-care 5 percent of the time, well within a normal mortal's acceptable level!)

My point is that couples need to agree on the amount or portion of time that is acceptable for them to be engaging in their own self-care activities. This may mean having their nails done, having a massage, shopping, golfing, hunting, or even playing cards with their buddies. The main thing is these periods need to be realistically negotiated and adhered to. The natural by-product of overdoing it is the sense that one partner is doing it all and the other is taking care of themselves and being selfish.

Too Much Focus on Work

Focusing on our careers is good thing. Bringing work home and then working on it to the *exclusion* of being with the family and helping with chores around the house is a bad thing. This will lead to resentment almost every time. Don't get me wrong, most successful people have times in their careers when they have to bring work home. If we are doing what we need to be doing at home, nothing is said other than, "Let me get the kids out of here so you can finish this." However, when we are spending more than about forty-five or fifty hours a week at our jobs, we are sending some pretty important messages to our mate. Starting off, we may be saying, "I would rather just be a provider." Most people know that work is easier than helping around the house with chores and childcare. If we aren't really the family type, we need to realize that we are copping out of our responsibilities at home. Perhaps this is not as much of an issue if we have a nanny or a stay-at-home wife. However, if our wife works as well, then it is pretty clear that we would prefer to make money and let them do the hard work of home and hearth. Cooking, cleaning, and nurturing children is very stressful and when you don't take your share of the responsibility, it feels like you are taking advantage of your partner and letting them do the hard work. Nobody likes being taken for granted or being taken advantage of. This usually leads to anger and frustration.

Sometimes being at the office is what we call escape-avoidance, an attempt to get out of doing something that we don't want to do. Sometimes, working is simply a priority problem.

Work is an important activity and most of us spend more time at our place of work than we do in our own home. Due to this, it is natural for us to develop relationships there. Both men and women develop deep emotional relationships at work. However, if your partner is talking about an opposite sex co-worker on a regular basis, most people start to wonder if something else is going on. I have a saying, "Reality isn't reality. Perception is reality." This means that you don't always generate resentment about what is actually happening. You generate resentment based on what you *perceive* to be happening or what you think is happening. It's still resentment.

When we have satisfying relationships at home, we rarely open up and have intimate conversations with opposite sexed co-workers. When we begin to do this, we are starting the process of commiserating with them or asking for their sympathy regarding our situation. When this is returned, because they themselves are not happy in their relationship, we start down the slippery slope of talking about how unhappy we are in our relationship and they are doing the same. Usually, the sense of having another person understand us and our emotional needs (especially the ones that are not being met at home), is a powerful source of connection. This leads to greater and greater levels of sharing and eventually feelings of attraction and love are generated. As would be expected, given enough time, a sexual relationship will develop. When this happens, the work environment provides almost all of the emotional and physical needs we have and thus we spend a good deal of time in this environment.

Some people are just workaholics. They tend to be this way by virtue of their temperament, come from the factory this way, or have shown this kind of industriousness their whole lives. Many times we find this trait attractive; especially if we were in a relationship prior to this where we wished that our partner had been more ambitious. It's just that many people assume that the workaholic husband will turn into the nurturing father once children come along. Pick your battles. If the rest of the picture is acceptable, you may want to just try and moderate this behavior and ask for some boundaries.

Many times, focusing too much on work is an artifact of problems with the relationship at home. We focus on work because it makes us feel successful and appreciated. We need this, and if we aren't getting it at home, work seems the most appropriate next best place. We also don't usually get criticized for "working." If we are tired of being criticized, this may be a natural outlet. Beware: whenever someone is not at home and too focused on work, resentment is not far behind.

Infidelity or An Affair

One of the most common reasons that couples enter into marital counseling is because they are headed for a divorce. Probably the most common reason that they walk through my doors is because one or both of them have had an affair. Infidelity has always been a problem, whatever the relationship. Be it a marriage, cohabitation, or just dating, one of the things that I set out to determine is whether this incident is due to emotional alienation or some other reason. Or if this is a onetime thing designed to get the others attention, help them exit an unsatisfying relationship, or ease some need they have that is not being met by the primary relationship.

The alternative is that this is not a onetime incident and is only the tip of the iceberg in terms of having affairs or cheating on their spouse. Is there a history, going back to high school, of cheating on their partner? Another question I need an answer to is, "Did this alternate relationship begin when the couple was doing fine but there was a need for excitement (thrill of the chase) or was there a need by the individual having the affair to find out if they were still attractive to others (self-esteem)?

Or, did this affair happen after years of feeling unappreciated and unconnected to their mate, leaving them vulnerable to seduction by a co-worker or someone online that made them feel attractive and desirable? Was it someone who stroked their ego or met some need that was not being met in the primary relationship? Was the affair an artifact of being hopeless about the marriage ever being what they wanted it to be and finding themselves having feelings for another, or was it an extension of prior behavior? Was it just a matter of getting caught at something that has been going on for years, no matter how happy they were in your relationship?" The other thing that plays heavily into the issue is how guilty or remorseful the individual was about having the other relationship. Did they lose weight and have a hard time sleeping because they felt remorseful? Did they experience remorse or a guilty conscience over their behavior?

Determining whether the behavior is historical or recent, something that makes them feel guilty or something that they have rationalized away, is significant. I have much less hope if this is a historical behavior. There is a saying, "Once a cheater, always a cheater." I tend not to believe this. The exception could be a few cases where this type of behavior has characterized almost every relationship that person has been in. In the great majority of cases, however, the behavior is more a function of being exquisitely unhappy in a marriage and not knowing how to improve it or feeling a great deal of resentment toward their partner.

My chances of helping a couple heal the wound of infidelity improve if I have a good understanding of why the behavior was occurring. The reason is this: couples can rarely go on and form a meaningful relationship after an affair, unless they get *closure*. They may go on and remain married, but they are usually paralyzed emotionally. They have lost the ability to connect intimately. As I have said before, "When we don't trust someone we start holding back part of our heart." Usually it is difficult for the wronged party to open up their heart and feel passionately toward their partner until there is closure or an understanding of, "My role in this and your role in this." The majority of people who have been the victim of an affair are left emotionally gutted. They feel betrayed by their most trusted ally. They need to know that it won't happen again. They want to open their heart up, but the heart is a funny thing. Sometimes we can beg it to forgive, but it just can't let the incident go, most of the time our hearts have a self-preservation mechanism that gets triggered whenever we get hurt emotionally. This means that we have a hard time opening up and sincerely feeling for the other person until the heart says it's OK and that it is safe to be vulnerable again. Hearts don't like to be broken. Early hurts in a relationship affect the hearts ability to survive a trauma such as an affair. *One never knows how much forgiveness resides in any given heart.*

For most people, there is a pathway back to my heart, to my bed. This trail involves not only what they need to hear to forgive; it also involves how they need to hear it. The level of sincerity, shame, the remorse, the tears need to follow. If these are not offered, if our partners do not make it right, do not tell us what we needed to hear and how we needed to hear it, the heart will reject their plea for forgiveness. I have been present during countless attempts to beg forgiveness. Most are sincere and once we discuss the resentment dynamic that brought them to that tipping point, there is closure, and there is forgiveness. Sometimes, however, I hear the words and I see the tears, but something is missing. They did not pass the test. Their heart did not accept the explanation or the amount of sincerity offered. Without this, there is rarely reconciliation.

Resentment Over Constant Criticism

For the person who is perfectionistic, critical, or controlling, there is a tendency to say, "Why don't you wash the dishes this way?" Or "Why do you vacuum like that? Wouldn't it be more efficient if you did it like I do it?" When this happens, the person thinks they are helping. They feel they are just offering advice. In reality, they are not because *what the other person hears* is, "That's not right. You're stupid. You're incompetent." They feel that the other is critical of them and is always trying to cut them down at the knees when it comes to feeling successful. It is hard to have swagger and self-confidence when we feel criticized. Due to this, there is a feeling that their mate is trying to kill any sense of accomplishment they start to develop. They start to believe that their partner wants them to have no sense of self-esteem; they want to keep them insecure and dependent on them.

Oftentimes situations tap into an individual's past; perhaps an early experience with a parent or teacher that the individual wanted approval from, a resentment dynamic is almost sure to develop. Once an individual feels criticized or corrected for the way they are doing things, it is sure to affect their level of connection and feelings for their mate. When this happens, as it does in all resentment dynamics, there are changes in the tone of the relationship. How can one feel sexually or emotionally open to an individual when they are so critical of them? More often than not, it will take marital therapy to help the person with perfectionism understand how the situation developed and how it is maintained. This means an understanding of their role in the dynamic and how it taps into their mate's fears and insecurities.

Sometimes criticizing one's partner has nothing to do with one's own feelings of perfectionism or sense of how things should be done. Criticizing one's partner may come from any number of other reasons. Perhaps that was what they saw growing up in their own family. Perhaps the individual feels that their partner is critical of them and they want to return the favor to let them know how it feels. Perhaps it comes not from a sense of perfectionism, but simply as a part of a person's temperament. They basically came from the factory as a rather controlling, critical, judgmental person.

No matter what is generating the criticism, it has to be altered in order for the relationship to mend. This means that the person has to understand the role their criticizing has on their partner's feelings of intimacy and how it generates feelings of resentment. Ultimately, it means they have to understand when they are being critical. Once again, reality isn't reality. *Perception is reality.* It is the person being criticized that needs to communicate to their partner when they feel or perceive they are being criticized. Often, this will be difficult for the person being criticized. If this were easy for them, they probably would have done this a long time ago. The understanding that they need to work through their own issues of how it makes them uncomfortable to confront their partner is very important.

Once a person becomes aware of when they are being critical of their partner and how this is affecting their partner's feelings for them, the true work begins. Initially, they need to work on becoming more aware of when they are criticizing or offering advice to their partner. This is either because they see the response of their partner or perhaps because the partner finally finds their voice or gets the nerve to say what they have wanted to say all along, for example: "Stop giving me advice. I already know the way you want me to do it. I like this way better".

Lastly, they really start to see improvement in their relationship as they practice their ability to take this knowledge from an unconscious awareness to a very conscious level. They have an ability to understand what they are doing and start to catch themselves *before they actually said what they wanted to say.* Once they start to catch themselves getting into the same habit, there is less saying, "I'm sorry. I did it again, didn't I?" As we all know, saying you're sorry only goes so far. People need to know that their partner is capable of change and of not being so judgmental or advice giving. This may take some assertiveness on the part of the other member of the couple. They may need to power through their discomfort and learn to say what they wanted to say all along. Silence does not help the situation. They need to be able to say they are feeling criticized or judged and they want their partner to stop. This helps the individual who is being critical to polish their understanding of what is considered judgmental and hurtful, and what is considered acceptable and helpful.

Resentment Over Making Decisions Unilaterally or Without Discussing Them as A Couple

Making decisions unilaterally means one of the members of the couple is making decisions on their own without consulting their partner. When individual's make decisions without consulting their partner (especially major decisions), they are sending a message about how much power they have in the relationship. When issues are resolved, they are put to rest. When a couple has thoroughly discussed an issue and made an agreement or a compromise, they resolve it.

When they can't resolve their issues, however, they start to lose hope about the whole discussion process and how important it is to talk about their issues. When this happens, when they realize that they can't stay in the ring and discuss their issues, the chances of one or both partners starting to make decisions on their own goes up. In other words, as things deteriorate between two people they start to make decisions themselves. They don't want to ask the other person what they think they should do as a couple.

Few relationships survive when one person makes decisions that affect the other and the household in general. When our partners are making major decisions, it feels like we have been cut out of the decision loop and have almost no control in the future of the relationship or where the resources are going. Not having influence raises anxiety and leaves people feeling disrespected.

For example: I have a couple I've been working with for several months, Becky and Chad. Becky and Chad have been married for fifteen years. They have two children; a son who's twelve and a daughter who's nine. The last five or six years have been very difficult and they have been close to divorcing on several occasions. Frequent arguments, awkwardness between them, and different parenting styles have lead to a sense of distance and harshness between the two. They are talking to each other but only about the children or specifics related to the running of the house. As Chad has said, "It feels like we are just roommates." As would be expected, most of the communication between Chad and Becky was strained and uncomfortable, as she described it, very "Businesslike." When they came to my office, there was nothing soft about their communication and each word seemed to have a great deal of anger and a hidden dagger behind it.

As with most of the couples I treat, on our first session I had both of them complete the Resentment Rating Scale. One of Chad's greatest sources of resentment was what he described as, "Becky making decisions on her own." Chad was a successful landscaper and Becky was a CPA with a large firm in town. Chad's job required almost no overnight travel. Becky's job required a moderate amount of travel.. Chad's resentment was centered on Becky making decisions to go to certain seminars or workshops without discussing this with him. As a seasonal worker, Chad was very busy May through October. During the winter, Chad had a much more flexible schedule and more time to dedicate to the family. When asked about the nature of the relationship and whether they had frequent arguments, Chad reported that the one thing they argued about the most was Becky's tendency to make plans without consulting him. The most recent episode resulted in a major screaming match and Chad left for two days. Chad stated that he had asked Becky on several occasions to try and take his busy season into account when she made plans to go to a training. Chad also wanted Becky to limit her workshops to weekends or only a night or two away from home. He reported that he harbored resentment about Becky coming home and "informing" him that she had booked a room at a nice hotel and that she would be going to a workshop (usually in a fun town like Las Vegas or Miami) to complete a training on "changes to the tax code."

Part of what made Chad resentful was that there was no discussion about the days away from home, but part of the problem was much deeper. Chad had always felt that he was a good, though impatient, father to his children. He would be the first to admit that he was more comfortable being the provider and allowing Becky to take care of the children. So, when Becky scheduled workshops out of town, Chad felt that he was being placed in a position of having to provide all of the childcare for a week. In addition, Chad was angry that Becky was unwilling to schedule trainings that were only one or two days long, rather than the weeklong junkets that he knew were only half-trainings and half-vacations.

Once Chad and Becky completed the Resentment Rating Scale they both started to realize they had a significant resentment dynamic with the trigger being the unilateral nature of decisions being made in the relationship by Becky, and then in turn, how Chad responded to her. Becky realized that she was resentful toward Chad for how much energy he put into hunting and fishing as well. Once they understood how these behaviors caused problems in the relationship, and how they needed to develop strategies for dealing with their differences while at the same time being sensitive to the needs of the other, things started to thaw between them.

Becky realized that Chad felt powerless; as if his contributions and time didn't matter to her since she would make decisions without consulting him. Once she realized that it would be in her best interest to discuss her potential training dates with Chad, things started to improve. Chad, in turn, changed the way he interacted with Becky and reported after three weeks that he believed that there were significant improvements in their ability to relate, as well as increased sexual activity. With increased awareness, things started to improve rather rapidly. By week six, the couple that presented themselves back in therapy was a new couple. Not only did they sit closer to each other on my couch, but the way that they looked at each other was different as well. Gone was the emotional distance between them as well as the tone of voice and contempt that characterized the first few sessions. They looked each other in the eye and made several positive statements about not only their hope for the future but their partner as well.

Resentment Because We Are Not A Good Match

Sometimes couples come to me on the verge of getting a divorce after fifteen or twenty years of marriage. After talking to them about the history of the relationship, it becomes clear that their marriage was *never* characterized by feelings of love. Rather, it was either a marriage based on convenience, security, sex, or a strategy to gain escape from a dysfunctional family. Usually after a brief courtship they moved quickly to talk of marriage.

All relationships change and people grow, but in these relationships this appears to be less tolerated and these changes only expose the relationship for what it is. What these individuals need to understand is that while these relationships can be saved, the ultimate question to be answered is, "Should it? Will it lead to the kind of marital satisfaction that they are both looking for?" Sometimes as a couple's counselor, I have the difficult task of telling a couple, "This is going to hurt, but you are not a very good match." We can polish these relationships with strategies for more respectful communication and more constructive ways of arguing. I can also focus on things that each member of the couple would like to do or could potentially do together. This sometimes gives the couple something to talk about and connect over. Examples might be if both individuals enjoy being outside, to discuss whether they should buy a trailer and start camping with their children? Should they book a weekend at a local city and spend the day exploring? Anything that will help them have at least one thing in common, something that they could talk about.

Couples need to look at the basis on which the relationship was formed and ask, "Is this going to get us where we truly want to go?" I do not come from the philosophy that it is always best to save a relationship; no matter what the cost. I would rather see two people go through the initial pain of a divorce (but ultimately find satisfaction and real love in the long run), than save a troubled marriage where the couple has almost nothing in common.

One of the things that I frequently find is that the reason couples don't get along is that they are simply a poor match. Remember, *time magnifies the degree of match in a relationship*. Let me say that just because a couple is not a good match does not mean they will end up in divorce court. Likewise, marrying someone who is a 90 percent match does not ensure marital bliss. However, my experience has shown that most couples experiencing happiness in a romantic relationship require a lot of hard work. More work than most people think, and a lot more than we think it should. Hence the term, "Love shouldn't be this hard." Well, yes and no. Maintaining love is quite difficult for most people. We see people who are quite happily married and are quick to point out that they would marry their mate again (pretty much the litmus test).

I believe that if you meet someone who is significantly like you in the important ways (spirituality, intelligence, sexuality, parenting, etc.) then it can be almost effortless to maintain a loving relationship. However, if you end up with someone who is not such a good match (but you love them), you may have to make peace with the fact that the strategies in this book are going to have to be mastered in order to be happy and you might have to work on your forgiveness and tolerance characteristics. In other words, you may need to be willing to work harder to gain the love you want.

Relationships can survive and even thrive with small amounts of differences between the couple. Occasionally, I will work with a couple for a few weeks only to come to the insight that they are a really a poor match. They don't complement or fit well with each other in the first place. Usually there is also a very limited degree of match as well; this means interest, hobbies, parenting, etc.

When two very different people find each other attractive enough to mate, but due to naiveté or the belief that "love will be enough," the differences come back to cause problems in the relationship. They cause problems in the frequency of things that the couple will argue about. A marriage can survive a certain amount of rocking the boat or arguing that occurs in a marriage or any relationship. I think it is obvious that the degree that we match in terms of beliefs about parenting, spending, politics, time, etc. (the extent that we see the world the same), decreases the potential for things we will have to argue about.

So what do I mean by match? *Match means the degree of overlap that occurs between two people on a set of characteristics, interests, and world views.* When I say characteristics, I mean temperaments and other personality traits. Are both of you kind, or is one of you kind and the other easily angered? Are both of you forgiving or generous, or is one of you generous and the other stingy? If you are, then there are bound to be disagreements. What if you find your mate attractive but realize they are not very smart? Research suggests that the average person marries someone within five IQ points of their own. Smart people are more prone to marry other smart people and vice versa.

Nowhere does match become more obvious than when it comes to interests. If one of you likes to go to the beach on vacations and the other likes to go to the mountains, there are going to be arguments. If one of you likes the city and room service and the other likes camping and hiking, there are bound to be disagreements. At an even deeper level, we wonder,

"If they don't like the things that I like, can they ever really understand me? Can they really get me?" Can we understand our mate if they are really different from us in terms of world views, politics, or even interests and hobbies?

Perhaps to a lesser degree, but certainly one worth discussing, is the degree of match when it comes to world views or politics. Sometimes people of different cultures find each other attractive enough to start a relationship. However, culture, with its many differences, can be a significant point of contention. Even if you have the skills to resolve your differences, sometimes families have issues with the different culture of your mate and attempt to drive a wedge between you. This can be very hard on a relationship.

What if one of you is green and the other uses a mixture of gas and oil to kill plants around the house? Or what if you drive a hybrid and your partner drives a Hummer? The difference in philosophy about how life should be lived is a very real one. People can be very passionate about the environment and what they think is important.

If the degree of match between two people is over 80 percent, then I believe that the chances of them being happy in a relationship go up dramatically. It almost doesn't matter whether they have the skills to deal with their disagreements and resolve their differences. There are so few differences that they just don't argue very often. The arguments they do have are usually forgotten before they have a chance to build up in the basement.

Match affects a couple on a very practical level as well; on a day-to-day level. *Nowhere is match more important than when it comes to our passions.* If your passions (be it the children, traveling, golfing or spiritual pursuits) are not shared with your mate, there are bound to be arguments and disappointments. If you are passionate about saving and you look at your investments every night to see how they have fared, you scrimp and save so that you can ensure a comfortable retirement for you and your family. Perhaps you have fears of not having security when you are older. You are passionate about saving money. But what if you are married to a spender? What if every cent that your spouse earns is quickly spent on some fleeting desire? What if you can't save because of credit card debt that was rung up by your mate? Your passion does not dovetail well with your mates. Difference is one thing, but passion is another. For many couples, love trumps whatever differences they might have. There are few things that can overcome the kinds of differences that passions elicit in us.

I believe that the degree of match of a couple equals the degree of flexibility a couple has as well. If my partner and I have the same world view about politics, spirituality, spending, parenting, hobbies, and sex, we are more understanding and hence "flexible" when it comes to our mates. We get them; we understand where they are coming from. This can't always be said when we come from different cultures or socioeconomic strata, or have different hobbies and interests. How can I be flexible and understanding if you are a conservative republican and I am a liberal democrat? If we don't agree on our interests, it is difficult to be flexible and understanding of the time and energy that sometimes come with these interests. To the degree that we agree on some arcane or rare interest, we increase the degree of flexibility even more. How forgiving am I going to be if I have finally found someone who enjoys my interest in arctic wildlife or Scandinavian beers? Pretty forgiving.

My experience is that the greater the degree of match between the two partners, the less energy will be required to sustain the sense of connectedness. However, to the degree that a couple is poorly matched (say 60 percent match or less); a good deal of energy will be required to maintain a sense of emotional connectedness. This is simply because to the degree that there is a good degree of match; there are generally fewer arguments and more activities in common which leads to more time together in general.

As I stated previously, time seems to magnify these differences as well. This means that if the differences are small after ten years, they will remain relatively small. However, if the differences between you are large, after ten years of being magnified, the differences will seem like a chasm has grown between you; a chasm of emotional distance fueled by the differences and ultimately the insight that you as a couple do not have a great deal in common.

When Our Partners Find Their Voice and Become Assertive

One of the things I see quite frequently in my practice are young couples that state that early on in the relationship they were quite happy. They go on to say that they were pretty happy for the first five or ten years of the relationship. Then they had children and subsequently, because of the organizational skills needed and the decisions the wife had to make because her husband was not home, the wife changed. The personal growth that women take from this and their own self-actualization cause them to develop confidence and self-esteem very quickly. Add a few successes and often we have a woman that has grown from being on the passive or dependent side in the early portion of the relationship to a woman who is more confident, capable, and much more independent than she was when she was younger. Not only more confident and in control of her life, but more *assertive* than she was when she was the 20-year-old woman that her husband fell in love with.

Please note: this does not have to be a significant problem for the relationship. If the husband is encouraging growth and is supportive of her new found voice, it can be very positive for a relationship. However, if the man in this situation feels that due to modeling or what he saw in his parent's relationship (perhaps a traditional 50s relationship), he likes the way the initial relationship worked, if he was comfortable with the dynamics that originally defined the relationship, he may not be happy with his wife's new found voice. The confidence and assertiveness that now characterizes the way she carries herself could pose a problem for him.

People rarely stay the way they were when they entered a relationship. Assertiveness is a good thing; however, there can be resentment or frustration if a relationship has changed and one of the parties was happy with the way that the relationship was when it started. There can be attempts to redefine the relationship back to the way it was when it started and when things were more satisfactory for them. The problem with this is that, as Martin Luther King stated, "You can't keep a man down without staying down with him." If you feel that your partner is not pushing you up, you may feel that they are trying to hold you back. If you feel that they are holding you back, it is sure to cause feelings of resentment.

Chapter Fourteen

SOME BASIC UNDERSTANDINGS ABOUT MARRIAGE THAT MAY HELP

Men Are Motivated By Sex

Men are motivated by sex. Well, most men are motivated by sex. At least this is enough of a rule that I can state it here. While this will come as no surprise to most, it is an important concept and one that must be understood in order for most couples to gain happiness. One of the unfortunate things (and one of the problems) about being so strongly motivated by sex is that men frequently mate for it. My sense is that the majority of men mate for sex. We don't want to feel guilty about sex; we want to have it on a regular basis. I don't believe that most men marry for children or to make their parents happy. I don't think that they marry for security, like many women do. I think they marry to increase the amount of physical intimacy they will get. Don't get me wrong, I believe in marriage and I think that marriage is good for men, but I don't think that is what most men are thinking when they decide to get married.

The thing about having sex is that when you share physical intimacy with a partner, you release more of certain neurotransmitters, vasopressin and oxytocin, that assist in the emotional attachment or bonding process. In other words, when you have sex with someone, you increase the chance that you will have feelings that you are in love with him or her.

There are problems with having sex before one is ready. There are, of course, concerns about becoming pregnant or contracting a venereal disease. However, from my experience the biggest problem with having sex before one is ready emotionally for it, is that you form attachments or bonds with a person. That is exactly what sex is supposed to do. It is supposed to assist in that bonding process. However, if the person is not the right match, you can start to bond with them prematurely. Likewise, if you engage in sexual activity before you are emotionally able to handle it and deal with the intensity of sexual activity and potential breakups, you may become depressed (because you will go through withdrawal from the neurotransmitters that the other person produced in your brain that made you feel good). Due to this, you may inaccurately believe that you are in love with them after all and cause you to marry the wrong person.

One of the problems with being so motivated by sex is that you have to make a good decision regarding whether or not you should marry someone. You have to be able to ferret out if this person is truly a good match? Are they an 85 or even a 90 percent match? If you can slow down to the point where you can keep your wits about you and determine whether the person you are dating is a good match for you, you increase the chances that you will make a good decision.

Instead of taking our time and going slow, waiting until we have someone that sees the world the way we do (who has an

85-95 percent commonality in the way we view the world), we frequently opt for mating due to physical attraction. Physical attraction is fine, but one needs more than a physical attraction to maintain a marriage. How many of us have friends that married quickly but whose relationship fizzled due to being only a 35-45 percent match in terms of intelligence, spirituality, ambition, parenting, or morals? These areas are where it is important to match. It is fairly common.

The problem with being so motivated by sex is that we mate for it. The great irony in this is that if you mate for sex, yet your partner is a poor match (anything short of about a 70 percent match), there are going to be a lot of differences that you are going to have to work through in order for this to be a satisfactory, monogamous, exclusive relationship. Basically, in order for you to be happy, much work will be needed. If you can't work through these issues, either because you don't have the tools or you can't get past the vastness of the differences, **there isn't going to be much sex.** Let me say it again, if you can't work through the differences and have a lasting sense of connectedness, there isn't going to be much sex; the reason you probably entered into the marriage in the first place.

What many men say is that the very reason they married (wanting sex) didn't quite materialize, and now they are angry and sexually frustrated because they wanted to have sex with their partner and that is not happening. Now they are confused. They don't know what happened. Men say things like, "We need to get you to a neurologist if you keep having all of these headaches." Not realizing that the headache is another way of saying, "I don't feel connected to you. I don't feel close to you or good about our relationship". Women don't feel sexual unless there is emotional connectedness, and men don't need it as much. So, when this need is not met, there are problems in the bedroom. Men (not always the most intuitive beings), are only guessing about what went wrong, how to get it back, and how to return their lives back to what drew them into the marriage in the first place.

Coming to the Y in the Road

Every day men and women come to a Y in the road. One direction takes them down the path to their own best interest and the other to their mate's best interest. "Do I do what is in my best interest, something that will bring me joy? Should I do something that I will enjoy, find interesting, stimulating, or fun? Or, do I do the responsible thing and go in the other direction toward the thing that is in the best interest of the family which will make my wife/husband happy?" Most individuals who enjoy a satisfying relationship with their mates want to maintain that friendship and the sexual relationship that accompanies it. If you have a good relationship, you give up a few things to preserve it.

If the relationship is not good and there is less and less sex in the relationship, less satisfaction, you start to ask yourself, "What should I do here? I could do what is in my mate's best interest, but that isn't going lead to them being any nicer to me, or to any increased chance of sexual activity. Or, do I do something that will be sure to bring me some satisfaction, but I will have to pay the price for emotionally?" What I find is that this dynamic (making a choice that is in one's own best interest) is what often fuels a couple growing more distant from each other. The decision is somewhat logical and rational. I understand where it comes from and how it is made. The problem is that when you start to do what is in your own best interest, you are setting yourself up to grow away from your mate. This is one of the things about the downward spiral that characterizes a resentment dynamic. You start to do things that are in your best interest, not your mates.

It is one thing to come to the Y in the road when there is a chance you might get sex or some of the things wanted from your mate. What is really significant is when you come to this point and there is no sex in your relationship or (for women), the sense that they are not getting the things they want from the relationship. Couples need to be aware of when they are coming to that proverbial Y in the road. Are they getting into the habit of doing what is in their best interest? Are they taking their satisfactions now in the short run, but leaving themselves open to criticism for being selfish? Be aware that decisions made based on feeling alienated, looking for an escape, or something that will make you happy for a brief period of time may work in the short run but not in the long run. In the long run, these decisions are sure to draw you farther away from your mate and reinforce their belief that you can't be the person that they can rely on in the future.

Why Most Women Lose Interest in Sex

Despite some social scientists attempts to paint men and women as basically being the same, I tend to disagree. I do not agree that humans are simply a male or female version of the same species. The reality is that we are extremely different. In my opinion, there is no way we are more different than when it comes to sex. Men and women, it seems, are wired differently. This will probably come as no surprise to most women. When we look at the outcome of engaging in sexual intercourse, the pictures are dramatically different. Men, not taking into account the responsibilities imposed on them by the court system, are able to engage in physical intimacy with almost no responsibility. Men's responsibilities are minimal after the act is completed. Women, on the other hand, have much more to lose in terms of personal freedom and much more responsibility should they engage in sexual behavior and become pregnant.

Historically, I believe that this has placed women in a difficult position. Unlike a man, who will not be forced by nature to undergo dramatic changes to his body and ultimately be given the responsibility for raising a child, women have evolved to look at sex differently. I believe that women enjoy sex as much as men do. Women in most cultures have gained the sexual freedoms that men have enjoyed for centuries. In essence, they now have the ability to decide whether to become pregnant or not. However, whether instilled by the 'Creator,' or as an evolutionary residue, the leftover instincts instilled over hundreds of thousands of years of mating, gave women an understanding that they have to be discriminating about whom they mate with. Women realize they need to be selective about whom they mate with for several reasons: they need to mate with a man who has the genetic endowment that will increase the chances of having healthy children. They need to be choosy about mating with a man that will be nurturing and helpful when it comes to providing for the needs of herself and the children.

Women (much like men) have always also engaged in sex for play. Once the decision to mate with a man and to form a pair bond has been established, they are still left with the decision, "Do I engage in sex with him just for the fun of it?" Herein lays one of the universes greatest mysteries (at least for men). Most women will agree that the actual decision whether to have sex with their partner is a complex decision based on several factors. What most women say is that their monthly hormonal cycle plays at least a minor part (for many, more than a minor part) in feeling sexual desire. Being on the pill can affect hormonal levels, so being on any type of oral contraceptive can lower (or increase in a few cases) a woman's sex drive.

Women produce smaller levels of testosterone than men do; however, the effect is the same. Testosterone increases drive and, in particular, sex drive. If a woman is complaining about decreased interest in sex, one of the things that I often recommend is to have her primary care physician check her testosterone levels. If a woman's levels are in the normal range, we know there is probably something else affecting her interest in sex. The thing about not being interested in sex is that if you are not interested, it becomes, "Just not that big of a deal." This is bound to cause resentment and frustration for their partner. Checking to make sure their hormone levels are in balance is a good way to show their partner that they are at least trying to get to the root of the lack of interest.

For many women, feeling well-rested and energetic versus feeling fatigued also plays a part in their decision whether or not they are in the mood for sex. This means that eating well and getting enough sleep to feel rested may improve one's interest in sex. Often when we are overwhelmed, we carve that little bit of extra time to do things out of our potential sleep time. Most people have an optimum number of hours of sleep. It is important to know this number because that is what you are going to need to feel rested and like you recharged your batteries. Without this amount of sleep, you will probably feel that your memory is not as good, you are tired, most likely irritable, and easily frustrated. If the reason that a woman does not feel interested in sex is due to being tired or fatigued, getting to the root of this is just as important. One of the other areas that may need to be checked at the same time that a doctor is checking a woman's testosterone levels are the possibilities of low thyroid or iron levels.

One of the biggest issues that affect a woman's interest in sexual activity is a sense of resentment or being tired due to an unfair distribution of chores in the home. If the distribution of chores, childcare, and providing income are skewed (even 60 versus 40 percent) there can be resentment over feeling like they have a lot more responsibility than their partner. This in turn may lead to resentment over one's workload and the resulting fatigue. When a couple comes in and there are issues of very little sexual activity, I naturally look at both resentment levels and the distribution of chores around the house. Even if the woman is at the right phase of her cycle and she feels emotionally connected to her mate, if a woman is tired then sexual activity is probably not going to happen. In fact, what is going to happen is that the woman will go to bed to rest and reject her partner's sexual advances (inevitably leading to anger, frustration, and eventual alienation on her partner's part).

Body image is also a significant factor for many women. Women who are self-conscious about themselves or their weight, who see themselves as unattractive, may not feel sexual. This is rarely an issue brought up by men. This is not to say that some men don't have issues regarding their partner gaining weight; some do. By and large, this does not affect a man's desire as much as women perceive it does. In essence, weight gain seems to bother women more than it does men. However, the result is the same. If a woman feels self-conscious when they get undressed, the chances are that they will not voluntarily place themselves in this anxiety provoking situation very often.

Stress can also be an important factor in whether a woman feels sexual desire. Men need to understand that stress from several sources builds up and eventually meets a critical mass. This critical mass tends to decrease a woman's sexual response. It is hard to relax and think about sex when there are other issues on her mind. Stress from work, finances, the house, and children all build up and produce a form of anxiety that makes sexual interest (and perhaps sexual response) more difficult. It is difficult to have an orgasm if you're not totally relaxed. If you are engaging in sex but not having an orgasm like your partner, it may be difficult to be too interested in the act. Unlike men, who often see sex as a stress reducer, women rarely feel sexual when their minds are on more pressing issues.

Taking antidepressant medications can also affect a woman's interest in sexual activity. Not all women experience a decrease in sexual desire when prescribed antidepressant medication, but many do. In fact, experiencing adverse sexual side effects is the #1 reason people discontinue or take themselves off their antidepressant medications. Not only do many women feel a decreased interest in sex, but many also report that it affects their ability to have an orgasm as well.

Now, after discussing all of the potential reasons that most women don't feel in the mood for sex, we come to the final reason. This final reason accounts for more than all of the other reasons combined. This is going to come as no surprise to women, but feeling *emotionally connected* to a man is hugely important and by far the biggest factor in a woman's decision whether or not to have sex for fun.

The reason for this is simple: having a man on top of a woman is an extremely intimate act. Nothing communicates emotional connectedness like physical intimacy. To engage in something so intimate, however, is difficult if she is not feeling emotionally close to her mate. When you are not emotionally connected to your mate or if you have a lot of resentment toward them, the thought of having a man on top of you (controlling you, setting the pace, and kissing you) is more than most women can bear. It makes them extremely anxious. The term that many use is uncomfortable. When this is the response that the thought of sex elicits, sex starts to diminish.

Most women want to be sincere and consistent with their emotions and what they are communicating to their spouse. When women are having sex with a man, they want to feel this is the message that they are communicating; "I enjoy this and I feel connected enough with you to do this." However, when they don't feel this way and have sex, they feel that they are only going through the motions. They feel they are sending the wrong messages about how they are doing as a couple. They communicate that they are responding to a guilt induction or out of responsibility. It is as though they are just laying there and letting their spouse masturbate inside of them, using them as a vessel versus making love. They feel degraded and used, not connected and close to their mate. This feels fake or insincere for most women and ultimately leads them to decisions regarding making changes in the status of the marriage.

What men need to understand is that if they want their wife or partner to be more interested in sex, they have to look at the whole picture. Is your partner depressed? If they are, what role are you playing in this condition? Are they overwhelmed and tired all the time? If they are, what can *you* do to make the chores more equitable? Perhaps if they were not so tired they would feel less resentment and have more energy. This does not always translate into an increased interest in sex, but it may improve your chances a little.

The single biggest thing that a man can do to increase the interest that his wife has in making love is much more difficult; that is because one has to truly look in the mirror and ask, "Are we connected?" Is she emotionally connected to me? Do my behaviors seem selfish or are they designed to be helpful to her and to keep us intimate? Is she resentful of me? When couples are more connected, when there is teasing, laughing, joking, spending time with each other, this is what provides the fertile field of emotional connectedness and sexual activity.

The Life Support System for A Family...Is A Couple

One of the problems couple's frequently complain about is their partner's tendency to hyper-focus on their children. This in and of itself is not unhealthy. In fact, it is quite healthy and the mark of a well-adjusted person. The problem is that every strength can be a weakness if it is overused. It was John F. Kennedy that said, "Show me a man that is a good golfer and I will show you a man that is neglecting something." In order to be good at something, you have to spend a great deal of time and energy focused on that activity. This same thing can be said of being a good minister, employee, and yes, even a parent.

In today's culture of keeping up with the Jones' and trying to provide for our children the way that our parents did (or better), we often find ourselves working 50-60 hour weeks and then trying to fit other things into our schedules. This can mean dance and music lessons, softball and soccer practice, and then the inevitable all day Saturday games and recitals. By the time we feed our children, run them to their respective practices, and get home, we have precious little time left to work on our relationships. But remember (and this may go contrary to popular culture, but it is important), the life support system for a family is a couple. Not a great mother or father, not time with the family or lots of money. Trust me on this. The thing your child most wants from you is to love their mother or father.

When we fly, the flight attendant says, "In the event of a loss of cabin pressure, a mask will drop from the ceiling. Parents should make sure that their own mask is in place before placing the mask on their children." There is a reason for this. You have to be healthy yourself before you can take care of your children. The life support system for a family is a strong couple; a couple that is emotionally connected and in love, a couple that a difficult child or mother-in-law cannot drive a wedge between. A couple that is strong and supportive of each other is a huge support to a family. When a couple is strong they talk to each other. In essence, the right hand knows what the left hand is doing. When they are strong they support each other. And they get their sense of connection and intimacy from their partner's (not the kids), so they don't need to be the kid's best friend. They can be what they need to be, their parent. It is through their relationship that they are fed and their batteries are recharged. When a person gets their needs met by their partner, they don't feel the need to hyper-focus on the children. They can't be broken apart with a divide-and-conquer strategy I see in some families. Couples that are connected clearly show their children they are the leadership of the household. Not mom or dad individually, but the pair-bond. I frequently tell my clients that they are the pond from which their children drink. If they become a desert, emotionally, spiritually, or physically, then they cannot provide their children with the emotional energy they need to survive.

This is important because many men and women feel they spend so much time at work and trying to satisfy all of their responsibilities that they feel guilty on Friday or Saturday night if they go out and have dinner exclusively with their spouse. They really feel guilty if they go on a vacation together without the kids.

As a therapist, I frequently have to give couples permission to take these times to work on their relationship, communication, sensuality, and maintaining appropriate attachment/bonding. There is a fine line between being selfish and providing appropriate self-care. While this runs counter to some couples' way of thinking, I believe that it is true.

What I am saying is that though there is a tendency for couples to say; "Hey, we work 50-60 hours a week. The kids are at school, with a sitter, or their grandmother all week. We need to spend as much time with them as we can during our free time. We had them; we owe it to them to parent them." I understand how important it is for parents to be there for their children. The caveat to that is in order to optimize how effective this parenting is, the parents have to be truly healthy, happy, and emotionally available to their children. Husbands and wives who are unhappy with their marital relationship rarely have the emotional resources to nurture their children the way children need to be nurtured.

Why do I say this? Because individuals who are unhappy in their relationships may be physically there for the children and may even be hyper-focused in an attempt to bring some satisfaction to their lives, but this is different from being in a happy, satisfying, monogamous relationship. When one is in a satisfying relationship, this frees them up to be centered, fulfilled, and to truly focus their energies on their children. Otherwise, their emotional energies tend to be focused on the logistics of getting their children to where they need to be and putting food on the table.

Don't make the mistake of believing that if your relationship starts to deteriorate you should fill the void with more focus on the children. This feels natural but it doesn't work. It is at these times that couples need to focus on their marriage. If you love your children, you will not focus on them during these difficult times. You need to give them the benefit of two parents that love them; a couple that is there for them. Emotionally and financially supporting a family has never been more difficult.

Two people who are in love and care for each other become the model that the children see for a healthy marriage. They become what their children will remember for how two people should talk to each other and interact. There are a lot of poor models out there that children see on a regular basis. Let your children see two people who are the leaders of the home. Yes, they argue, but they are respectful and resolve their differences. They carve time out for themselves. This is not selfish. This is the very self-care that is important in maintaining the integrity of the family. When couples carve time out for themselves, it communicates that each is still important.

Once children sense that you and your mate are intact, you can make difficult parenting decisions. Many of these decisions will not be popular, but they need to be made. I see this in the healthiest couples. They stay connected because they carve time out for themselves. They take vacations without their children sometimes; even if some naysayers judge them. Look, everyone knows what kind of parent you are anyway. Trust me. People can see if you are selfish or selfless by all the other interactions they have with you. Trust yourself. Carving out time for the couple will pay dividends both when the children are in the home and when they have moved on. Work on maintaining the connection and the rest will follow. Your children will see you as a leadership team; not two people who share the same space but whom they can play one against the other. They will know that you're too tight and too connected to even try that strategy. They know that you talk every day, several times a day, and that they can't get anything past you. This holds your children to a different standard. They know that they have to take responsibility for their own behavior because there will be no way to escape or avoid it. And they will realize early on that they can't drive a wedge between the two of you. And don't worry if you and your spouse have been alienated in the past. The perception that you and your spouse are "together on this" can still be instilled in one's children; even if there have been periods where the both of you haven't been close.

Remember, if you are successful in your quest to stay connected, you will stay married. Nothing is more important to the health of your children than staying married. When researchers ask young girls why they didn't get pregnant or experiment with sex early in their teens, their response is consistent. When girls have a father at home that they have a good relationship with, this keeps them from being needy for acceptance and affection elsewhere. They also say that they would not want to lose their father's respect, so they make difficult choices to maintain their father's approval. Carve out time for your marriage; it will pay dividends in the long run. Carve out a date night. Carve out time away from the children to walk or talk. Couples need to maintain communication so that their children know they truly love them.

A continuum exists in human nature that measures a person's tendency to do what is in their best interest or the best interest of others. This continuum is selfish versus selfless. Selfishness is on one end of the scale and selflessness on the other. We all have to ask ourselves when we come to this fork in the road, should I do what is in my own best interest, or should I do what is in my children's, spouse's, or parents best interest?

Where I see this cause a problem in some marriages is that many parents don't see the healthy place in the middle where self-care lives. Self-care proposes that 85 to 90 percent of the time, we do what is in other's best interest. A small portion of the time, however, we need to do what is in our own best interest.

Making time for our mate is important because free time (the time we need with our partner) does not occur in nature and must be carved out. Finding a few moments or an evening here or there for our mates is difficult because there is always something else that will take that time. There are always children, the house, work, our parents, etc., that can (if we allow it) take up this time. It is in the carving it out and making it a priority that we show our mate how important this time with them is. The fact that we carve it out makes it more valuable and hence more special to our mates. My point is that parents need to find a balance between their own needs, the needs of their mates, maintaining the standard of living they have chosen, and the relationship that feeds and nurtures their children. This is a difficult balancing act for some however. There are, of course, our own fears of being seen as selfish or not a good parent. There are also the all too frequent guilt inductions offered by grandparents and co-workers. It seems there are always parenting experts out there willing to throw out statements such as, "Wow, you went to Florida without the kids, must be nice." Don't take the bait. Only you and your mate know how much time you need together in order to maintain your sense of emotional connectedness and intimacy.

Chapter Fifteen

DEBBIE AND ALAN

D ebbie is a teacher at a local elementary school. Her husband, Alan, is a successful sales rep for a furniture company. Debbie and Alan have two children; Kayla (six) and Brandon (four). Debbie and Alan both work long hours at their jobs. Once they are home, however, they tend to spend most of their free time with their children. While early on in the relationship there was a good deal of dating and spending time together, after children arrived, this went by the wayside. This was more by Alan's choosing than Debbie's. Alan had been raised by divorced parents. While Alan was able to see his father on weekends, he was often disappointed by his dad not showing up on the agreed upon night. Due to this, Alan was adamant that he was going to be a good father and be present in his children's upbringing.

Debbie loves her children as well and enjoys spending time with them. However, what was revealed in therapy was that Debbie was resentful about the lack of time that she had with Alan alone. Debbie and Alan had been married for five years prior to starting their family. Early in the relationship, Alan and Debbie had traveled extensively and, though they worked long hours, they had weekends to travel and spend intimate time together.

What came out in therapy was that Debbie missed the meals together with Alan and the sense of connectedness that came from these intimate moments. She also realized that she was experiencing growing feelings of being, "Third on Alan's list," behind his job and their two children. Alan admitted that he, too, missed the time that he and Debbie had together; particularly early on in the relationship. He was torn, however, between his need to spend time with Debbie, and his need to be a good father.

After this was revealed in couples counseling, the focus switched to seeing Alan and Debbie separately. Therapy was focused on two main areas; helping Debbie to communicate what she needed from Alan in terms of treating her as a priority and what she wanted the picture to look like that would be a win/win (a home life that was both an acceptable amount of time for her and Alan being happy about the amount of time that he was spending with their children). Therapy for Alan was focused on helping him find a better balance in his life. Alan focused on working through his anxiety about fears of being perceived as abandoning his children and giving him permission to carve time out for Debbie.

After a few weeks of individual therapy, Debbie and Alan came back together for more couples work. Debbie was relieved to see that Alan was open to the idea of spending more of his time with her and slightly less time with their children. They agreed to set up a date night every Friday to try and spend more quality time together. The agreement was that one of them would make plans (arrange reservations, decide on the restaurant) and the other would be responsible for arranging a babysitter. After working through Alan's initial fears, the couple came back to therapy a few weeks later.

The couple I saw after eight weeks of therapy was dramatically different from the couple I saw on the first night. Not only did they sit closer together on my couch (the first barometer), but they touched each other and looked at each other differently as well. No longer was there a coldness and distance between them. They were teasing each other and looking at each other with a smile on their faces. What they communicated was that through carving time out for each other, they realized how much they missed their dates, and the time that they had just for each other. They stated that they would talk to each other more during the week and started to e-mail and call each other again during the week to chat or talk about what they wanted to do on their date. This was important, because they had originally reported that they had stopped communicating with each other almost altogether (except for when they had to talk about the children). Not only were they going on a date and leaving the kids at home, but their children also reported that they were enjoying spending time with the babysitter, playing games, eating pizza, etc. This relieved Alan's fears that his children would do a guilt induction or be traumatized by the two going out and not including them. Alan was happy to report that he and Debbie enjoyed a glass of wine when they went out and had made love later that night after returning. This was also an improvement since the couple both admitted that their sex life had suffered along with their relationship.

A follow-up appointment three months later found the initial improvements to be intact and with a number of other areas of their lives better. Not only had they continued to carve out every Friday night for themselves, but they had also agreed to plan a vacation to Jamaica without the children. Alan also reported that there was an unexpected dividend to the investment that he and Debbie had made to each other. He reported that there were fewer behavior problems with the children, and their children seemed to be happier and getting along better as well.

Chapter Sixteen

M AINTAINING INTIMACY

E arlier in this book we discussed the meaning of intimacy and how easy it is to disturb the sense of emotional closeness within a relationship. Maintaining this state of intimacy is quite difficult for many couples. What I find is that intimacy is fragile. Once earned, the trust that comes with this level of connectedness can easily be damaged.

I grew up in the thumb of Michigan and there was a neighbor family of three boys who frequently argued; calling each other "a—hole, and stupid fu—ker." There was what would be considered physical and emotional violence between all of the members of the family.

In some families, this would lead to alienation, lack of trust, and unwillingness to help each other after one of these altercations. Not with this family. Barely a half-an-hour after a big fight, one or the other would say, "Hey, do you want to shoot baskets?" and they were off playing and laughing again.

These cases are a bit of an anomaly but the point is this: some couples, like this family of three boys, understand the frailties of human nature, love each other, and forgive the other's mistakes and go on. Each couple I see is somewhere on the continuum of forgive and forget resting on one end of the scale, "You screw me one time and I will never ever forget or forgive" or on the other, "Yes we fought, but do you want to take a walk." The ability to see the frailties of human nature in the world of people living 80 or 90 years and trying to maintain marriages of 50 or 60 years is daunting. People make mistakes. Some have the ability to get past them, however, and some (like a puppy with a sock) hold on to them and can't let them go. No matter how many times we try to hide the sock under the couch, they find it and bring it back out to chew on it.

Arguing

One of the things about arguing for a couple is that most don't do it well. They are not good at arguing. Most people are uncomfortable with arguing, so they don't do it if they don't have to. This means they avoid conflicts or go into denial and stuff their issues, holding them in because of the discomfort associated with sharing them with their partner. Instead of approaching their partner with small issues and dealing with them, "Hey, honey could you not drop your towel in the bathroom. I don't want to have to pick it up." These individuals don't want to be seen as difficult or "rocking the boat." Or, they avoid conflict because they don't want to stress an already damaged relationship. These individuals avoid the problem and act like they will go away. They, of course, do not go away. They are stuffed and come out later.

The problem with stuffing issues and holding them in is that once an argument has started and feelings are hurt, what does come out is often pretty powerful. When that happens and we vent too much anger, what comes out is either too powerful to be productive (remember all issues are resolved between calm and agitated) or is so scattered that it is hard to focus on one issue in order to get closure. To continue the example, "Well, you drop your towel in the bathroom and expect me to be your maid, you continue to charge your cigarettes and pop on your Visa card, and you're never around on Saturday when I need help around the house."

The reason for this is simple. Typically, people like to see themselves as nice. They don't like to get upset. Being upset is bad. Raising our voices or becoming anything other than in control is a bad or negative thing. It affects our self-concept and self-esteem. We have fears that we won't be liked or that we will be perceived as a bitch or an asshole. If we have spent the last twenty years of our lives developing a self-concept or persona of being a nice or kind person, starting an argument is inconsistent with our character; to engage in anything that makes us look that way makes us uncomfortable. So, how do nice people argue? How do kind people communicate that they are unhappy in the workplace or in their relationships?

What I tend to see is that rather than vent their feelings of frustration, disappointment, or resentment, nice people tend to stuff them. When I say stuff, I mean that (much like an old jack in the box), we tend to cram all of the things that irritate us and then forget them rather than deal with them when they are experienced. After all, would a nice person want to feel like every time they interact with their spouse, they are complaining? That would make them the very thing that they swore at an earlier time they didn't want to be. So, they stuff away.

We rank irritants. On a scale of one to ten, we rank the things that bother us. A two irritant might be someone pulling in front of us on the highway without turning on his or her blinker. A five irritant might be expecting someone to be home at a certain time and they are two hours late. Each person has a very intricately worked out scale of what bothers them and what *really bothers them.* What nice people normally do, rather than tell someone that they are upset with them at the time of the infraction, is tend to let this build up or stuff the issue. What this means is that inside the issue box we have a two-point infraction (dropped their towel on the floor of the bathroom), a seven-point infraction (forgot anniversary), a pair of fives, and a four. Now, when something triggers a reaction or they have reached a critical mass of annoyance and frustration, they finally let it out. The nice person blows. What comes out is not an appropriate response to a wet towel being found on the bathroom floor. What comes out is a rage at the person being so inconsiderate and adolescent, to without thinking drop their towel for someone else, in this case, "the maid to pick up." What comes out is the pent up, seven, four, pair of fives, and a three. It all comes out. They have no control of the matter.

This overreaction often takes on a historical quality because it brings up all of the infractions that have been experienced or tolerated for the last six months or since the last blowup occurred. But, rather than being civil and logically communicating one's frustration and disappointment in a rational and respectful way, it comes out angrier than one would normally expect taking into account the nature of the infraction.

When this happens there is a tendency to try and hurt, bully, or threaten the other person. We use foul language; we yell and scream. How else can we communicate our aggravation?

The problem with this scenario is that we risk the chance by handling ourselves poorly so that in the course of a five minute argument, we may undo all the healing we have done in the last six months; all the connectedness and closeness we have managed to develop or nurture in the last few months. *You can undo in a five-minute argument with the use of harsh or disrespectful words what it has taken you a year to heal since the last argument.* People need to realize that words hurt more than physical blows. People tell me this all the time: "I would rather be hit than be talked to the hurtful way they do to me." This is because we can undo all the healing in a few moments.

Intimacy, as I have stated before, is a state. It is a circumstance or condition that exists in every relationship. Most couples know when they are in this emotional state because they are not walking on eggshells; there is a sense of interpersonal comfort between them. This is the state of intimacy. And as a state, it is a living, breathing entity. It has a life of its own. It changes almost daily. What intimacy does is serves as a standard or level of connectedness that we have with another individual. As we trust them and feel close to them, we realize that we could open up and share with them. We show them those parts of us that are broken. We are vulnerable with them. Not only the parts of ourselves that we are proud of, but those parts that we don't show everyone because we don't believe they will honor those insights. If we trust someone, however, we are placing ourselves in a situation of being vulnerable.

This state of intimacy opens us to being hurt if we expose ourselves. But it also opens us to a greater level of connectedness and can increase the bond and love between two people. It is a sense of commonality that exists nowhere else. We have a natural drive to connect with people, especially the people we are having sex with, the people we are physically intimate with, and the people we love. We crave this level of connectedness where they can read our minds and (with a look) can communicate almost any thought. They can often understand our emotional state simply by looking at our faces. They intuitively know by the tone of our voices what our mood is. Are we happy or upset? Most people long for or desire to be in this state with their mates. And that is what intimacy allows us to do.

My point here is that maintaining intimacy is difficult. It is a delicate state. Nothing affects the state of intimacy like arguing does. Or at least like destructive arguing does. In most cases, **civil** arguing might actually *improve intimacy*. It may improve intimacy because when we argue in a civil and respectful way, we communicate that there is hope we can be mature adults when we are upset or angry. This is huge because almost every person I treat has a long history of being in relationships with people who overreacted or damaged relationships with their response to not having things the way they wanted and the resulting blowups that followed. Unless they grew up in such a home, most people have a hard time imagining a long-term relationship where the intimacy level in a relationship is limited by the bi-monthly blowout argument.

I was in session with a couple several years ago and was struck by a situation that occurred. We were working on resolving a conflict they had argued about on the previous week. It was a simple issue having to do with a closet and whether the wife would clean it out, move some things out of there, and where she would put them (with specific focus on not putting them in the husband's office). This couple went round and round. He brought up issues of how things usually end up on the kitchen table, how the wife puts his things where he can't find them, and some vague references having to do with the husband not liking the wife's parents; in other words, a typical argument for this couple and many others.

I refocused the couple; informing them of their tendency to get off-track and hence their inability to resolve the issue of the closet. With this in mind, they tried once again to find a solution to the predicament of what gets moved, by whom, and where the stuff would go. I thought that the wife made a pretty good proposal for what she would do to resolve the problem. The husband seemed to not have heard. He continued on his argument having to do with how he couldn't find things after she moved them, how he couldn't trust her, and the fact that he disliked her parents. I stopped the session to bring attention to what the wife had said and how perhaps he needed to listen for an acceptable answer and agree or accept a proposal when one was offered.

How often is this us? How often do we not listen when our spouse offers a perfectly acceptable solution, but we are so busy forming our next argument or beating the same old dead horse arguments that we don't hear a solution? Sometimes we need to be able to stop ourselves. We need to be able to hear our partner when they articulate a pretty acceptable compromise or an agreement that both can live with.

When the Sex Starts to Decrease

One of the things about being in a long-term relationship is that couples have the chance to go through a number of phases. One of the most difficult phases, for men in particular, is when a relationship has lasted a year or two and there is a good deal of familiarity (meaning we have gotten to know each other and we are really comfortable). This is a nice place to be for most couples. However, there is one particular problem for men at this phase, namely sex. As everyone knows, early on in a relationship sexual activity is passionate and frequent. But what happens when it starts to decline? How does each party approach the issue?

Men are motivated by sex. We are not the noblest beast in the field. We are, however, the way we are. I think if most men had a choice, they would decrease the whole testosterone level a notch or two, decrease their sex drive, and the amount of time they spend thinking about sex. If they could, I believe that most men would decrease their sex drive just so that they could be more productive and concentrate better. However, when men get used to a certain frequency of sex it is hard for them to understand why things changed. Men frequently don't understand what happened and why things have to change in the sexual arena. How did they go from sex on a four or five times a week basis, to now having to beg, do guilt inductions, or back rubs to get it? We initially believed that we might have found one of those fabled women who genuinely had a strong sex drive; perhaps one to match ours, or as we have heard from some friends, outdo even **our** interest in sex.

Since most know these women occur only rarely in nature, we have probably ended up with a normal woman who has a strong interest early on in the relationship but starts to diminish after the comfort level rises, real life kicks in, and the love hormones start to decrease. The problem is that many men feel that rather than this being about the woman's comfort, it is more about the realization that she has finally caught him and now he can't leave anyway. He is in love, but he realizes that he is in love with a woman that now does not want to have sex as much as he does.

Now what happens? What happens when we are thinking that we may have sexual activity four or five times a week, but ends up being closer to once or twice? Well, this brings on a new phase and new problems. Most notably is the frustration and pouting that men frequently start to exhibit when they are disappointed and irritated because they are not getting the sex that they want. (Trust me; there is nothing sexier than a grown man pouting because he wants sex.) This is probably (and hopefully) the first time that the woman in this situation has seen this type of behavior from him. She was perhaps hoping that he was one of those guys that was mature and understanding about the nature of relationships and one who would take the ebbs and flows of interest in sex in a more adult manner.

This is usually when the resentments start for many men. They start as sexual frustrations. The problem is that once men are sexually frustrated, other smaller things start to bother them and build into greater issues than they really are. They show up on our radar as a 7, 8 or 9 when they are really a 2, 3 or 4. The good news is that given a little emotional connectedness or physical intimacy, these issues tend to go back down to where they belong.

Frustrations start a cascade or cycle of resentments that often feed on each other and fuel greater and greater levels of dissatisfaction with what was probably, at least initially, a good relationship. When men don't get sex for a while and they are used to it, they start to overreact and become concerned that they will get even less. Focusing on other hobbies, pouting, doing guilt inductions, and pulling away due to resentments, leads not to greater levels of connection, but lesser. Ultimately, this leads to less sex, primarily because women don't feel close to them and because women want sex to be spontaneous and not planned (i.e., three times a week).

Most men report that they value sex a great deal, but that physical touch of almost any kind, including hugging and hand holding, are almost as good as sex. These are almost as important as sex because they make clear that their mate finds them attractive. My message here is that while having sex may count as 100 points (100 intimacy points) in your partner's eye, sometimes a hug (80 points) or taking their hand in the car and telling them you love them (85 points) are almost as satisfying to them as physical intimacy. These actions go a long way; especially when there is a disconnection in terms of how often one partner wants sex. The key is to find a way to let your partner know that you are only interested in non-sexual touch, not something that will ultimately lead to the bedroom.

Why Making Corrections to an Intimate Relationship Causes So Many Problems

As society advances, it seems that what it expects from marriage evolves or changes as well. Our expectations about what we demand from a marriage go from basic to more sophisticated. At one end of the spectrum is a business partner. Essentially we are raising kids together; trying to find a way to survive to more complex and sophisticated expectations. On the other end is what society now almost demands from a marriage. This means best friend, lover, and soul mate.

As the expectation for the marriage goes up, the business of the marriage becomes more difficult to perform. It becomes difficult to confront our partner, to say those things that are bothering us. In a business relationship, it is different, if you are a partner in a business, you are able to talk as business partners do. This is what we need to change to survive. We can say, "This bothers me about the way you are doing this, how can we do it differently?" We survive. That is harder to do when you want to maintain a best friendship, when you want your soul mate to still care about you. It becomes more difficult to confront someone the more you *care about them*.

But today's couples don't want marriages of convenience, nor a business relationship or an arranged marriage that allows them to survive. Marriage has changed, culture is changing. If you were my business partner, it would make me uncomfortable to confront you, but not so uncomfortable that I wouldn't tell you that you were doing something that bothered me. So, if we had an issue, I would confront you. It would make me uncomfortable but I could do it.

However, if you are my lover or my best friend, *confronting you on that same issue really makes me uncomfortable.* I have a hard time confronting you now because I don't want to lose access to that level of connectedness, that friendship. I don't want to lose that level of comfort with you. If you are my business partner, I don't care. I would prefer not to have to confront you and it will make me a little uncomfortable, but I will do it. In business you might get upset, but you will come around. We're both in this to survive.

All relationships require corrections and adjustments. Usually, the longer the relationship, the changes that have to be made by both parties are more significant. Sometimes just initial tweaking is required; sometimes they are significant mid-course adjustments. Children come along, health problems occur, and life-changing insights that call for a significant change are activated. This becomes an issue of how do we perform corrections on an intimate relationship that requires corrections?

All relationships require correction. Long-term friendships are no different. But in friendships, we have the option of leaving. All of us have done this. A friend did something that we didn't like. We either wanted them in our lives so we forgave them, or we said, "Well that is just the way they are." Rather than confront them and tell them what they were doing that bothered us, we probably just dropped them as friends; but you can't do this with a marriage.

One of the biggest problems with most marriages or relationships is that the two people within the relationship don't tolerate the discomfort of arguments well. The other thing is, as a society, people try and keep up with what they think they are supposed to have in a relationship. What we are told by the media is that we have to be soul mates and always be happy with each other. What we see on TV are relationships where we have to get along. We have to be nice. And if you don't do that, you are a bad person, if you are not nice, you may be rejected or be abandoned; all because you don't get along well with others.

This is irrational. It makes it difficult to be in a relationship because this belief sends the message that we have to get along all the time, and if we argue or have heated discussions, that is a bad thing. Nothing could be further from the truth. We are shown that arguing is a bad thing and doing it means that we are a bad person. Not understanding that constructive arguments create a better relationship.

People are living longer and relationships are expected to last longer. The expectation about how satisfying our marriages have to be is also on the rise. As expectations go up in relationships, we have to do *more* of the corrections to maintain it, not less. The risk of losing the relationship goes up and what we stand to lose goes up. We don't make the corrections because we don't want to argue and be seen as difficult. We also don't want to do the confronting, or make the corrections, because to do so makes us uncomfortable. There are now more threats than ever before to the marital relationship. Maintaining that pair-bond gets more difficult and staying monogamous becomes harder.

I have developed a strategy that works well when couples need to tell their partner something that they fear will make them upset. I call this strategy, "The Therapeutic Hug." A therapeutic hug means that one partner approaches the other and says, "I need to give you a hug". Now this may be interpreted as, "Oh great, what now?" After giving the partner a hug (or in some cases after the hug, but when still holding them), we tell our partner what is bothering us. I have found that it is hard to be upset with our partner when they are hugging us and telling us at the same time, "Will you please put your dishes in the dishwasher instead of the sink when you are done with them?" This strategy is effective at communicating what is causing resentment. The risk of course is that if you don't communicate it, in essence if you stuff it, it will build up and undo your emotional connection.

Keeping One's Agreements

Needless to say, getting in the ring and agreeing to a compromise loses its power if we don't keep the agreement on Monday that we made on Sunday. We have to be willing to make agreements that we can keep, and we have to be willing to keep the agreements we make. Nothing will kill hope quicker than an agreement that was quickly settled (and your partner knew that you just wanted out of the ring), but not upheld later when the issue finally reappears. When this happens, our mates wait until the issue comes up again to see, "Will you keep your agreement or not? Will you abide by your word, or is your word not worth anything?"

When someone's word or promise is no longer binding, the remaining partner knows that it is time to exit the relationship or start looking for alternatives that are more honest. Mature individuals need relationships that they can build a future on. We need hope that if we are going to go through the discomfort of arguing about something, then the outcome or agreement better be binding. If we are in a relationship with a partner who makes agreements and then does not keep them, we realize that they are either not honest enough, mature enough, or too selfish to ever do something that they don't want to do. We lose hope. Hope is an important emotion when it comes to long-term relationships. If we lose it then we start to make exit plans because we need to feel that we are in a relationship with someone who can match our level of compromise and change.

Why Is It Important To Resolve Our Differences?

What portion of the differences between couples can be resolved through discussion? What portion can be resolved though compromise, through negotiating, and finding the middle ground? It probably depends on the individual or which couple you are talking about. My sense is that for most couples about 70 percent of all issues can be resolved. This means that if the couple can get in the ring and discuss the issue, if they can be civil and productive in their discussion and not hurt each other, then they can probably resolve 70 percent of all their disagreements.

What that means, however, is 30 percent of all issues don't have a compromise and don't have a win-win; there is not an agreement that can be reached between the two individuals. Healthy relationships can tolerate a limited degree of unresolved issues (perhaps as large as 50 percent); if there is a good degree of match and both parties are able to provide the other with an element of emotional connectedness. But, if there is not a good degree of connectedness, match, or chemistry, it is difficult to determine how many issues left unresolved will cause a total loss of hope. Couples need *hope* that they can resolve their differences. They need to believe that if they work hard enough they can learn to compromise or talk through their issues.

There are always going to be some issues that are never going to be agreed upon; whether you go to the mountains or the beach for vacation, for example. Thirty percent of a couple's issues left unresolved are still a significant amount of difference, resentment, and disagreement. ***This means we have to leverage the heck out of the 70 percent that a couple can resolve!*** It is important to understand that the number of issues a couple does not resolve actually depends on several factors. The degree of match that a couple has is a huge factor in how many issues they argue about. The degree of flexibility and maturity level of the two individuals in a couple also plays a significant role in how many issues go unresolved.

As we have established, couples have to get in the ring to resolve 70 (or whatever number) out of every 100 issues. ***If they can't get in the ring they resolve 0 percent of the issues.*** Resolving none of the issues leaves a couple vulnerable to significant amounts of resentment building up. Couples have to learn to resolve that part of the disagreement they can, because they need to save a space for those issues that can't be resolved. The basement is only so large.

Some issues may never have a resolution. Some issues are too painful and bring up powerful emotions. Examples are credit card debt, drinking, flirtations, disappointments, and differences in parenting. Most relationships can absorb a certain amount of unresolved issues and the resentment that they generate. But as I have said before, no one knows exactly where their partner's critical mass of resentment and alienation lies. How much forgiveness and mercy is their partner truly capable of?

The Problem with Frequent Arguments

Arguably, one of the most damaging types of disagreement is the frequent tiff or spat that some couples find difficult to avoid. By spat, I mean that there are regular small arguments or disagreements which characterize the couple's time together. These arguments don't always necessarily lead to alienation or the breakup of the relationship, but they cause problems in terms of the couple's sense of connectedness or intimacy.

The problem with frequent arguments is that they rob the relationship of the long-term feeling of being close to each other or feeling emotionally connected. By this I mean the sense that, "*We have been getting along well for the last month and have not had an argument to send us backward*; back to some previous and less satisfying level of trust and intimacy. Once a couple has experienced or tasted a certain level of connectedness, it is frustrating to settle for some lesser level of happiness and contentment.

Little spats or disagreements can send a couple backwards in terms of how happy they are or how close they feel to their mate. If these arguments occur too frequently, they can affect the general health of the relationship. These conflicts or disputes often occur so frequently that the couple does not have the time between quarrels to heal emotionally. This has to do with the general forgiveness capacity of the couple. With time to heal, the couple will probably be back to previous levels of connection in most cases (depending on the couple, and each couple knows how long it takes before the smiling, laughing, and responding sexually returns) within three to four days. However, if spats or disagreements occur more frequently than every three to four days, the couple will not have sufficient time to heal between arguments and the relationship suffers at a deeper level.

While differing from the types of arguments that cause resentment, these spats usually keep a couple from feeling connected. They don't usually cause the relationship to breakup, but they can cause disruptions for periods of time. What I usually see as causing these spats is different from the dynamic that was discussed in the first part of this book. These are not generally the result of a resentment dynamic. Rather, these quarrels are usually due to one or both members of the couple's idiosyncrasies; an individual's unusual reaction to a situation, personal peculiarity, or behavior; in other words, a quirk. We all have quirks or things that are a little odd about us. These may be reactions to germs or little rituals that we have to follow. They may be issues having to do with money or feeling controlled. The list is endless. However, these generally don't change, even with therapy. What I aim for is awareness of one's idiosyncrasies, and therefore being more aware of when we are responding to them for us and being less sensitive to them with our mates.

Let me use an example. Sharon grew up poor and her family did not have much money for "extras." Due to this, she does not like to make a purchase that is impulsive or not necessary and she also has issues with feeling that she does not bring enough money into the household (that she isn't pulling her weight). What might happen within Sharon's marriage is a situation where she is out shopping with her husband, Steve, and he makes an impulsive purchase.

Steve is a successful businessman and makes a comfortable income. He works hard and feels that he should be able to make small purchases without feeling bad about them or (more importantly) being made to feel guilty. In this relationship what often happens is that Sharon, with her sensitivity to money issues, may make a statement to Steve about his impulsive spending, or say, "Why do you need that?" This, in turn leaves Steve feeling like Sharon is the mother and he is the ten-year-old child that is quickly spending his allowance. Steve becomes frustrated and shuts-down emotionally because he does not feel he did anything wrong. Sharon is not aware of how important her issues with money are and has no knowledge of the passion she has for honoring her idiosyncrasy of being frugal. Steve frequently makes a sarcastic remark about the incident and retreats emotionally from Sharon. The result is the same in many other situations. Steve feels he has been unfairly made to feel like a child and Sharon does not understand why he had to make a hurtful, sarcastic remark.

What I try to do in therapy, is bring a person's idiosyncrasies to an awareness level instead of being at an unconscious level. If our mate knows that we grew up poor and have issues having to do with spending money, they will be sensitive to this (as our little quirk) so that when we get upset over small non-necessary purchases, they don't become frustrated and feel like an impulsive child with their spending habits.

We Need To Be Listened To

People need to be listened to. The problem is that some people are not particularly cut out to meet their partner's needs. Yes, we need to listen to our co-workers. Yes, we need to listen to our children. But if there is one thing that our partner's really need from us, it is our ears.

Not just listen to them, but to really hear them. They want us to (and hear me here) commiserate. This means empathize, sympathize, console, try to understand, and support. NOT, try to fix, say, "Get over it", or just shrug our shoulders and say, "That is the way it is." This is not what most people want. They want to be validated; they want to be told that they have a legitimate and well-founded reason for being upset, period. Just that; just to be listened to and to have us nod our heads at the right time; to be looking at them so that when they look at us, we are looking at them. Not the TV, not out the window, but at them. This says, "I am listening to you."

If I can offer some words of counsel, most people do not want our advice or for us to tell them what they should do, or how to fix it. This, in fact, is the last thing our partner's want from us. If we do this, they will not come to us in the future with the things that are burdening them or bothering them. We will lose this opportunity. Some of you may be asking yourselves. OK, so I will lose the opportunity to listen to my partner tell me the same story over and over about some woman at work that I don't even know or about how her mother gets on her nerves and criticizes her. Boy, aren't I just missing out on a good time. Well… Actually, you are.

One of the most significant things that you can do for your mate is to simply listen to them and be a good sounding board. All of us have things that bother us. If we have control of these situations, they cause us discomfort. If we don't have control of them, they really cause us discomfort. Listen to your partner; even if this is the tenth time they have told you a story or complained about someone at work. People appreciate this and your stock will go up. It will go up because you will look supportive and mature. That is because supportive and mature people know that listening is a little thing that means a lot.

Now, if you want extra credit, you may want to go even further. You may want to ask questions. Why would you want to ask questions? By asking questions about something, we give people permission to go further and to expand upon what they were discussing. This says to your partner, "I am OK with being a sounding board that lets you vent your frustration with this situation." By asking questions, we give them permission to continue, to go further. They will look at you and feel that it is OK to continue and go further. This is important because they need to vent but they don't want to impose or bother us. It's better to get this frustration out than stuff it and make them keep it in. When they stuff their problems because they don't have an outlet, a number of things can happen.

They may let their worries build up and become overwhelmed and depressed. Therapy is healing; partly because it allows a person to vent or talk about what is bothering them. This makes them feel heard and understood. One of the things that can happen when we have something on our minds and we don't have an outlet to talk to about it, is we go looking for an outlet. We look for someone to talk to.

With online connections like myspace.com and facebook. com available, there are a lot of opportunities to talk to people via the Internet. And do you want to know something important? When we talk to people and they listen to us and really hear what we are saying, we start to really like them. We start to have feelings for them. (This is why people start to have feelings for their therapists.) We start to compare our mates to them and often our mates come up short, because we have found another person to listen to us and hear what we are saying. If they sense that this person does not try and solve their problems, judge, or criticize them, this is extremely attractive. "Wouldn't it be nice if I had a person like this around all the time?"

If you don't have someone at home to listen to you, you are vulnerable to seduction by someone who will listen. All people need this. It validates them; it says they are important and the things that are on their minds are important. So when we don't have a person at home that will listen to us, we start to look elsewhere for a sounding board. This may mean that coworkers or people at work will now get the opportunity to get access to their inner world or those inner concerns that they have. When we start to talk to others about what is on our minds, our fears, worries, concerns, and those things that need to be said, we open a portal; an entrance to our inner world that can allow others to enter. This is one of the most common ways that affairs happen; when the need to talk about things is not available.

The Two Pillars upon Which Love Stands

My philosophy is that the two pillars upon which love stands are **Trust** and **Respect.** This is a very important concept. These two things need to be present for love to grow and be maintained. This means that we have to *trust* the person we are in a relationship with and we have to *respect* them, or ultimately we will fall out of love with them.

It was one of my favorite authors, Stephen King, who wrote "Love and lies don't go together, at least not for long." Mr. King was absolutely right. The lies will inevitably build up and drain any trust or confidence that we might have had in our mates. Without confidence in their word, love, at least true love, cannot last.

Trusting someone means that when they say, "I am going to do something, _____ (fill in the blank)," they are going to do it. "I am going to pick up the kids after school, get a job, make dinner, etc." When they say they are going to do something, I believe they do it. When I say "A" you get "A," not "B" or "C." You will get what I said you would get. Not only does it mean that we trust them and believe that they will do something, there are several other messages embedded in this behavior.

First, they are an adult versus a child, where you can't be sure if they will actually do something or not. Adults actually do what they say they will do. Second, it means that you can take it off your "to do list" and know that it is still going to be done. This is a relief. Lastly, it means you can trust "their word." Now in relationships, being able to trust your partners "word" is huge. If you can't be trusted, or if you can't trust your partner to do what they say they will do, **then you question everything.** You wonder about everything you ask them to do. Will they do it? Will they remember to do it? Will you have to prompt them or gripe at them to do it? Without the ability to trust your partner, you lose hope.

Hope is important in terms of seeing a brighter future with our partner. Without hope, we lose our sense of optimism that things will be better and that we are in a relationship with an adult, or someone who is capable of being the kind of partner and parent that we need to shoulder the other half of the load. That we are evenly yoked, or that we will only have to do **part** of the job of raising our children, running a house, paying the bills, etc.

Trust implies not only that they will do what they say they will do. It also implies that they can be trusted with what they say. If people lie, or if they stretch the truth or embellish, the same dynamic applies. If our children tell lies 5 percent of the time, then we question everything. We question the other 95 percent of the things they say. This takes a lot of energy and eats away at intimacy. Our partners also feel misunderstood and frustrated when they feel that 95 percent of the time they **were** telling the truth. But there is an old saying in psychology, "Anxiety comes either from a task we are unprepared for or a future that is uncertain." It is hard to base a long-term relationship on the uncertainty of things happening or not happening, or believing or not believing what someone says.

I think another reason that trust is so important to a relationship is that is serves as the basis for our ability to leave the household at the beginning of a workday. If I trust my mate because they are responsible, I have less fear that they will cheat on me or have sexual relations outside of the relationship. If I can't trust them in our ordinary world, how am I supposed to be secure in my belief that they won't have an affair? We have to trust our mates or there will always be a lingering fear in our unconscious that they might be plotting something that will shake our sense of security. We realize that if we can't trust our mates, we are opening ourselves up to being hurt or having our hearts broken.

Not only is there the issue of not knowing if you can rely on your partner, there is the whole issue of their anger when *they* feel you don't believe them (because this time they *were* telling the truth). Inevitably, this leads to comparisons between their behavior and that of a child's. I don't know how many times in therapy I have heard, "It's like I have three children." Nothing will anger a man or woman quicker or make them feel more disrespected than being compared to a child.

One of the biggest reasons that trust is such a significant issue in a relationship is that if we don't trust our partner, we start to hold back part of our heart. We become guarded. What I frequently tell my clients is that if we don't trust our partner, we start to hold back either a little bit, a sizable chunk, or a big part of our hearts. We may not be leaving but we spend parts of our day wondering, "How much of my heart should I be holding back?"

We ask, "What if I put myself in their hands and they betray me?" We start looking at the decisions they are making on a day-to-day basis and use those decisions to decide if we should be holding back a great deal of our heart or only a small amount.

This means that we hold back access to our inner world, how much we allow ourselves to care for them, to plan on a future with them. We start to prepare ourselves for the possibility that our trust will be betrayed. We don't want to be blindsided and caught unprepared. Because we know at some deep level that if we can't trust them, we are eventually going to be hurt. In order to decrease this sense of impending hurt and in an effort to minimize the pain, we start to hold back our love, our caring for them. We become guarded. We know that if we open our hearts to them and care for them, trust them, we can be hurt. This is our way of minimizing the hurt. We fear what might be coming. When that day comes, we want to be in charge or in control of how much we are hurt; in essence to minimize the chance that we will be devastated. We know we need to be there for our children, to continue to be able to work. We know that if we limit our vulnerability to them, we can only be hurt a little bit (or at least that is what we tell ourselves).

We dream, however, of a relationship where we don't have to hold back *any* of our heart; a relationship where we trust our partner with our best interest, with our hearts. One where we don't expend energy on looking at their daily attitudes and decisions to decide how little of ourselves we are going to open up, how little of our hearts we will risk; one where we trust them implicitly; one where our energies can go to productive efforts rather than self-protective ones.

Trust is important because if we can trust them to hold true to their words, we can trust them with our hearts. We can trust them with our love. We open up our inner worlds to them and become vulnerable because of this. But if they have shown that they cannot be trustworthy with small things, then we know that we should hold back a commensurate amount of our hearts.

Our partners may or may not sense that we have started to hold back part of our hearts. Just because a person holds back part of their heart, it does not necessarily mean that they are planning on leaving their mate. It simply means that they have fears that their feelings may be in jeopardy, and that they should preemptively go into self-preservation mode. When we start to hold back even a small amount of our hearts, we start to fantasize about how nice it would be to be with someone we could trust. When greater amounts of our hearts are held back, individuals start to actually make contingency plans just in case they are betrayed. Once again, this does not necessarily mean that they are actually leaving, but they want to be prepared just in case. Once a critical mass of distrust is met (or holding back a significant portion of one's heart), most people start to actually begin to put together a war chest, or financial stockpile in order to be able to survive the upcoming life trauma.

One of the final reasons that trusting your partner is so important is that in order to enter into a truly mature relationship, you have to be able to tolerate the sense of surrendering to another. What I am saying is that there are different levels of marriage. There are **basic** marriages all the way through **mature**, almost enlightened marriages. I am not implying that this type of marriage is the only type that can bring happiness. I have seen marriages that are quite some distance short of this enlightenment, yet much better than each person saw when growing up, hence, something that they are both happy with. Much like how there is no **one** religion for everyone, there is no one marriage style for everyone. You have to find out what you are most comfortable with. No matter what type of marriage you end up with, **trust** is going to have to be present or you will have difficulty sustaining your relationship.

Why Respecting Our Partner Is So Important

There are several reasons that respect is so important in a relationship. It forms one of the two pillars upon which love stands. We know it is important because when it is not present, when we lose respect for our mates, we start to fall out of love with them. This occurs for several reasons. If we don't honor or respect our mate, it shows. Not only do we not respect them, but ultimately we show our disrespect or contempt for them.

Respecting something implies that we treat it with a certain amount of reverence or admiration. It shows that we admire our mates. Our mates communicate that they respect us by taking our feelings, needs, thoughts, and wishes into consideration. How do they do this? By asking how we feel about something; they validate our feelings and don't criticize us. They empathize with us and validate our experience without being critical. They ask us questions and listen for the answer. They don't interrupt us. They then communicate their respect when they seek to understand us better and by taking our feelings into account when they make decisions.

The very nature of respecting someone says I am paying it attention and attending to it. Thus, disrespecting someone is consistent with ignoring, neglecting, being indifferent to, or disregarding them.

It is through respecting others that respect is returned to us. By paying attention to them we are maintaining a dynamic whereby through being responsible, accountable, and reliable, we show that we value and respect our mates. If, however, they don't act in ways that allow us to respect them, inevitably this will be apparent in the way that we talk to them and treat them.

We all know couples that admire and value each other. This becomes quickly apparent; primarily in the way they talk to each other. In comparison, we also know couples who are doing just the opposite. They are disrespecting their mates. We realize how unhealthy their relationship must be in order for them to treat their partner the way they do and how unhealthy their partner must be to allow themselves to be treated in such a fashion. *Relationships become unbearable when we don't feel we are being treated with respect and no well-adjusted person can tolerate being talked down to or ignored.*

What It Means To Truly Be Connected

Intimacy means opening up. It means sharing not only the good things that lurk in our inner lives, but also what we have done wrong and what mistakes we have made. We know we have access to our partner's intimae when they feel safe enough with us to share the less than perfect aspects of themselves.

Having a deep level of connectedness with another person is a natural drive for most people. When we have this level of intimacy, we actually recharge our batteries by being close to them. This is true of men and women, but I will admit that it is especially true for women. Women love to feel really close to a man because it invigorates them.

The problem is that it takes two people to maintain the state of intimacy that I discussed previously. If only one person is well-adjusted enough to trust a person and let them in, this will not be sufficient for intimacy to be maintained. If one person is using drugs or is resentful, this will not be a truly intimate relationship. It takes two people both opening up to enjoy this state.

How do you know when you are in a truly intimate relationship? How do you know when you are both feeling close and comfortable with each other? The truth is that early on in a relationship, *you can't*. When couples have just started to date, their relationship radar is so messed up by the influence of sex and the neurotransmitters that are released, they really cannot discern, "Is this is the person for me or not?" True intimacy is best revealed over time. Once the blindness of the early part of the relationship has been replaced by the realities of each other's weaknesses and brokenness (in other words our warts), then we can see the truth. Only then can we determine whether our potential partner is secure enough, able to open up emotionally, and able to trust enough to take a couple to the level of intimacy that we all dream about.

Intimacy is the Energy that Fuels a Relationship

Intimacy is the energy that fuels a relationship. By fuels a relationship I mean that it maintains it and helps it grow. Without intimacy relationships dry up and die. Men and women differ significantly when it comes to intimacy however. Women are primarily fueled by Emotional intimacy (capital "E") and by sexual intimacy (small "s"). Men are fueled by Sexual intimacy (capital "S") and by emotional intimacy (small "e").

I frequently hear women say to their spouses, "I don't feel close to you." Only when a woman articulates this or I help a woman communicate this can she leave a trail of bread crumbs to her spouse about how to change this. Literally, showing her partner, "This is how I get my cup filled; this is how I feel connected to you; this is what you do that makes me feel close to you." Men don't frequently understand the importance of this sense of connectedness. When men finally understand the importance of intimacy and have the understanding on how to provide it, it becomes easier to do.

Perhaps it is when men take time away from activities they enjoy and give it to their mates that makes them feel like a higher priority. Now this time may not be as important to a woman if a man has to be told to carve out time with them

or else. Women prefer that a man intuitively reads their minds and sense's their needs (shows that he is in tune to her needs). Men can learn how to provide their mates with more intimacy and learn how to connect. Even if these skills are not possessed by a man naturally, these are skills that can be learned. Men who intuitively sense their partner's needs get extra credit.

Often, women communicate a feeling of having experienced a bait and switch because the very energy that goes into a relationship early on, which makes possible the state of intimacy and connectedness, isn't maintained after a year or two. Therefore, the connectedness starts to deteriorate. To stay connected requires a good deal of energy. When we inject connectedness or intimacy into a relationship, it acts as fuel. Things start to change between the couple. When we feel close to a person and able to communicate with them at a high level, we open up energy that flows toward that person. Most people report that it is the same for their partner. When they have open communication with their partner and they feel close to them, they get more energy coming their way as well.

The Importance of Talking

We can't underestimate the importance of keeping the communication channels open. Things really start to deteriorate in a relationship when we lose the ability to talk. We need to be able to talk to our mate. In particular, we need to be able to talk about our interests. We have to maintain the ability to talk to someone on a daily basis about not only the things we are worried about, but also our interests, things at work, or our hobbies. If we don't have this ability or if we lose this ability due to our alienation, the door is open for someone else to fill that void. The opportunity arises for another individual to be the person that our mate goes to talk about work concerns, to bring their successes to, to talk about "how they found a great sale today," or to talk about "the fish that got away." When we become alienated from our mates, they no longer want to come to us with the things that make up their world. Let's be honest: when we put together the little things that people talk about most of the time (jobs, interests, the kids, etc.), these little things make up 80 percent of our lives. If we only talk about the 20 percent (that makes up the house, groceries, etc.), the logistical issues of a home, we lose the ability to talk to them about the things that really interest us.

People need to feel appreciated as well. They need to be told by their partner they appreciate what they do for them. Being able to communicate, telling their partner they think they are lucky and that they appreciate what their partner does for them is difficult. This is hard for men to do in particular. My sense is that it is slightly easier for women. It is important to be able to tell your partner that you appreciate what they do for you. Men really need to hear that what they do is appreciated. They need to know the things that they do around the house are noticed and valued. I know that a lot of women feel like they shouldn't have to tell their mates they appreciate that they took out the garbage, that they noticed they mowed the lawn. What I often hear is, "He doesn't tell me thanks for doing the laundry." Many people find it difficult to say they value what their partner does for them.

Remember, when you lose the ***interest or the ability*** to talk to your partner, you may not be at the point of divorce, but you can see it from there.

Do We Always Have To Be Right?

Sometimes people get caught up in the issue of having to always be right; the person who has all the answers. While seemingly attractive, this can play against you when you are married. Yes, you want your partner to trust you and see you as intelligent and competent. It is also important that you communicate to your partner that you trust them. To communicate that you believe in your partner enough that you would take their point of view over your own says, "I would rather have a relationship with you, than be right this time. I would rather have a relationship with you, and send the message that I respect you, than to prove that I am smarter than you." These moments occur throughout the day. When you come to an intersection, do you turn right or left? Which is the quickest way home? By choosing your way home they get the message that they are not trusted as competent and intelligent. What is more important? Getting home two minutes faster by taking a right turn (the way you think is shorter), or sending a message about how your partner might be right and how they have a good sense of direction?

Is this you? Does this describe some of your interactions? Sometimes when we come to that intersection, we should say, "Well, it might very well be that way. You are good with directions." or "Well, let's try it. You are more familiar with this area than I am." What are a few minutes? As the commercial goes; Time it took to get home, a few minutes longer; Gas to go an extra few blocks, 21 cents; Sending a message that you trust your mate, PRICELESS.

Nobody likes a know-it-all, and we pay a high price for maintaining this dynamic. We pay a price because we either get into a competition with our mates over who is smarter, more competent, or a better parent. We send a hurtful message about how we think it is more important to be right in a situation than to honor our relationship. In other words, it is more important to be right than to be happy.

The Reservoir of Anger and Our Radar

For many individuals who are in a long-term relationship, the dynamic discussed in this book will develop. Essentially, the couple started out happy but then things started to be revealed as issues of contention. One or both of the parties do not have the tools in their toolbox to deal with these issues, so these gradually built-up over time and ultimately drew the couple apart. When this happens, there is a phenomenon that starts to occur. The term I give this is, The Reservoir of Anger. I help my clients to picture this reservoir as a large ball of a black substance, which is located underground, but its topmost edge comes very close to the surface.

The reservoir refers to the building up of a large amount of anger generated from an inability to resolve differences. These anger reservoirs build up over time. They are frequently generated by anger we have with people in past relationships, but they also hold some of our current relationship's unresolved anger.

When we leave old relationships, we gradually become less and less angry because we are no longer subjected to the reservoir on a daily basis. This does not mean that the reservoir is gone or has somehow been drained. Another term for the reservoir I am referring to is one's baggage. This means the pain and unresolved emotions we brought from our previous relationships. We have all heard the term, "I like them, but they have too much baggage." Of course, they have too much anger from their past relationships which bleeds into the present relationship and affects it in a negative way.

Everyone has some baggage or a reservoir that can cause him or her problems. The predicament is this: since the reservoir is so close to the surface, there are things that other people do which *taps into our reservoirs and make us angry.* Before

I go further, however, I must describe another phenomena closely related to the reservoir. This is the issue of our radar. Everyone has a radar screen that we scan throughout the day. Radar is really just another way of saying that I am scanning my environment for threats to me. Everyone has seen a TV program or movie where the submarine captain or the air-traffic controller is looking at this screen. They are supposed to be picking-up threats to us; threats like missiles or bombs. Our radar is set to pickup a different threat however. **Our** radar is similar and is supposed to pickup threats to us, things that we are sensitive to.

Since we are sensitive to certain issues or situations, our radar beam is not slowly rotating around the screen, around the center source. No, our radar is on high alert, meaning that you can't turn the knob any further. It is literally screaming around the screen. The more sensitive we are to an issue or the more sensitive we are as *a person,* the faster the beam goes. We all know people who are way too quick to take offense or are too sensitive. These people's radar beams are a blur, because they are going so fast. The reason that our radar is out there in the first place is to pickup threats. However, when the beam is going too fast, it starts to pickup false-positive readings. This means that it is picking-up flocks of birds; it is picking-up trees moving in the wind, etc. **Our** radar is so sensitive that it is picking-up chatter or things it is not supposed to be picking-up.

When we are this sensitive, we start to watch and become so sensitive to being hurt or to things that people are doing that we lose perspective. Here is where the two issues of our reservoir and our radar come together. *When we lose perspective on how sensitive we have become, we overreact to things*.

We overreact because the reservoir is very close to the surface. We think we have buried it, but it is close to the surface and hidden by a thin veneer of earth. The trouble comes when someone does something that shows up on our radar as a threat to us. This is when (like an oil well that has hit the mother lode) our anger comes out as a geyser. What has happened is someone has tapped into our reservoir. They have tapped into our frustrations or the fears developed in childhood. They have tapped into what we are sensitive about, due to how people have treated us in past relationships. Now, as it spurts forth its emotions from past relationships, we lose perspective on how serious the infraction or insult was because we are so sensitive.

What kinds of things are found in the reservoir? The things that most frequently come to mind are issues such as being sensitive about substance abuse, being treated disrespectfully, or being cheated on. Other examples include being sensitive about another person's impulsive spending or too much focus on friends.

If you are sensitive to being treated poorly due to your father's or ex-husband's drinking problem, when you enter into a new relationship you see small indications of problem behaviors such as keeping alcohol in the house or becoming intoxicated at a party. But rather than say to yourself, "Hey, all he did was get a little too intoxicated at his friends party" (considered by most to be a minor problem), your radar senses this as an indicator of a much bigger problem and taps into the reservoir of alcoholism and years of disrespect, arguments, and financial insecurities generated from your first marriage. Viola, you get angry. Much more angry and insecure than you should be, taking into account the nature of the infraction. He tapped into your reservoir. Many people don't know that they are sensitized to certain behaviors or that they have a reservoir of things that they react so strongly to. This means that they have blind spots of which they are unaware.

The problem with having a blind spot is that we don't know that we have it. This makes it all that much more of a problem. This sensitivity causes problems in relationship after relationship, but we are often not aware of them, so they continue to plague us, making us wonder if there is something fundamentally broken about us and if we will ever find the happiness we desire. People frequently turn to their friends for advice, but friends are trained to be supportive of us, not to confront us on how we are being too hard on our partner or how we are too sensitive.

One of the most powerful things about working with a therapist is that they can help people to understand that they are sensitive to certain things and to identify their blind spots. The significant thing here is that you take responsibility for yourself and those unconscious mechanisms that have been developed to protect yourself from threats. This may mean looking in the mirror at your own issues and what you bring from your upbringing or past relationships. Long-term relationships take a forgiving nature. Nobody wants to live in a relationship with someone who is sensitive. It feels like we are always walking on eggshells, waiting to break through the eggshells, and offend you.

When we work with a therapist and start to understand what we are sensitized to, we can be more aware of it; especially when we sense that our buttons are going to be pushed or that we are getting agitated, fearful or anxious. This means not living in denial, but rather being aware of not only what we are sensitive to, but also why we are so sensitive to begin with. Armed with this information and awareness, we can now start to not only be aware of our radar but how far we have the knob turned and what it is picking-up. "Should this bother me? How much should I be worried about this behavior? Is it an indicator of a much bigger problem or is it a frailty of human nature?" Not a deal breaker, not a character problem, just one of the ways that the person in your life is not perfect.

How Much Resentment Does It Take To Fall Out Of Love?

How much resentment does it take to fall out of love? The reason there is no precise answer is because there are so many variables and no real equation to plug them into. Variables like how long the resentment has been going on, how forgiving is the person who is harboring the resentment, what is the nature of the insult, is it an affair, or is it a partner who is working too much? What are the people around you saying? Are they saying get out when you can or are they saying, "I would stay and work it out"? All of these issues and probably a hundred more are at play in the problem.

What I don't believe is up for debate is the matter of why do people fall out of love. The answer for me is clear. One of the things that, as a student of human nature, I have been trying to understand my whole career is, "Why do people stop loving each other?" Isn't this the holy grail of marriage counseling, to understand the reason why couples that have been happily married for ten years suddenly tell their friends they are unhappy and have decided to split? Why is it that a couple can be happy for years and then decide that they no longer love each other?

One of the things that I commonly find in the breakdown of the feeling of being in love is the issue of critical mass. I am referring to a buildup of resentment over a long period of time. This build up may take several years or even longer. Rarely do I see couples who are truly in love take less than at least two years to break down the feelings of being in love. The cause of the resentment and how much hope we have about the situation getting better also plays a huge role in how much the critical mass builds. There is also the matter of what decreases the mass, meaning things like vacations or finding another thing (such as children) to focus their attentions on. Certainly, a case can be made for being able to connect emotionally (laughing, joking, teasing), for even a brief period of time, that makes us feel closer to our partner. This may, for at least a brief period, help us to forgive our resentments. But nothing lasts forever and eventually our resentments, like old debts, find us.

Couples routinely come to me and say that things changed in the relationship after two or three years. There was a decrease in the sense of being high emotionally when in the other person's presence. There was a moderate decrease in sexual activity from several times a week to two or three. And there was also a moderate decrease in the need to be with the other person for extended periods. In general, the rush of feeling like you are in love starts to diminish.

The good news is that the number of individuals that communicate this is relatively small. Rather, what I hear much more frequently is that there were feelings of love felt mutually for several years. More often than not, this feeling survived the childbearing years and added credibility to the idea that the couple was a fairly good match and not the poor fit that they communicate about each other once the relationship is in peril. More often than not, they were a young couple that had done a fairly good job of finding a mate and fell in love. However, what they say is something happened to the relationship and things started to deteriorate. Most couples are able to understand their experience to this point and a bit further. They admit things started to change and that the number of arguments started to increase. After that, most are only able to say, "We grew apart." They are unable to articulate the existence of a resentment dynamic, the exact behaviors that triggered the resentments, and where they are in the continuum of alienation. What I have found is that 90 percent share the same experience.

This is where most couples start to feel like they are falling out of love with their partner: when almost every interaction they have with their spouse leads to negative emotions and hurt feelings; when the feeling of being in love chemically is gone; and when the hope of being able to change the behaviors that are affecting the couple's sense of being connected is lost. This is when couples start to fall out of love. It does not usually happen quickly but gradually, as illustrated by the continuum of alienation mentioned earlier. Eventually, the individual is left with the sense that they no longer love their mate. When this happens, they are left at a crossroad. Do they attempt to get the feeling of being in love back? Can it come back? Most have no idea where to start.

So the issue of how much resentment it takes before someone falls out of love is a valid one. I believe it was Dr. Daniel Simmons who said, "How many times did the Titanic have to cross the north Atlantic before it got in trouble?" Obviously, the answer is only once. It _may_ only be one more time that you alienate your partner before they lose hope or start to fall out of love with you. One never knows; your critical mass may be at the lip of the caldera; ready to pour out of the volcano and overpower your ability to manage the problems in your relationship. Or, as for many couples, there is still time (though the degree of intimacy and connection has been compromised) to figure out what is triggering your arguments and returning your relationship to its previous state.

There has been research done which suggests that the average woman leaves her husband six times before she actually moves out for good. This suggests that it is a process. There is a progression of emotional disengagement. Over a course of time, a woman starts to make peace or gets used to the idea of moving on. No research, that I am aware of, has been done which has focused on how many times a man leaves his wife before he actually has had enough and leaves for good. Many people who come to me for help did not realize where their partner was in terms of their critical mass of alienation, not knowing where they were in the process of walking out the door emotionally.

Reality Isn't Reality, Perception Is Reality

I have a saying . . . reality isn't reality, perception is reality. In long-term relationships, we create our own reality based on how we think or feel we are being treated. Reality or what is actually happening in a relationship is not what matters. What matters is what we perceive is on. This can be, depending on how close we are to seeing reality or how sound our information is, either very accurate or very inaccurate. If we don't see reality for what it truly is, we often make up information to fill in the gaps. This, as would be expected, can add a toxic or poisonous element to any relationship.

One of the things that counseling does is to help each of the partners see things clearer. It often helps to explain irregularities in behavior so that inaccurate conclusions are avoided. The point isn't, "Is my wife having an affair?" The point is, "Do I think my wife is having an affair?" If an individual finds his wife closing her phone or laptop as soon as he walks into the room, he can become suspicious. If she has been working late and not around much, he may believe "she is cheating on me." (When, in fact, his wife is planning a surprise 40th birthday party.) With these "perceptions" in his mind, he may start to back away emotionally to protect his feelings. In other words, he goes into self-preservation mode. The husband's withdrawal may lead the wife to feel that she is not trusted.

Whenever we don't have all the facts in a situation, we tend to fill the voids with our own version of the story. We have a need to organize our thoughts so we can make sense of them. If our partner is doing something that we are having a hard time understanding, we start to form our own version of what really happened. Sometimes a normal activity (golfing, as an example) does not raise suspicions, however, if a friend plants seeds of suspicions, "Is he really going up north to golf?", you may begin to wonder.

To ground ourselves in reality, clear and frequent communication between spouses is essential. When you start to sense something about your spouse that doesn't add up or you don't understand, start a conversation—or get help. You don't want to start down the slippery slope of interpersonal alienation based on something that a friend said or something your partner did that you misinterpreted. Once it has been revealed that you overreacted you may not be able to recover. "Oops, sorry, my mistake," may not fix the hurt feelings. At the end of the day, your partner is going to ask, "Why did you make that assumption? Why didn't you just ask me?" Making erroneous assumptions becomes easier when you're not speaking to each other. When you're not communicating you are vulnerable to these kinds of misunderstandings.

Understanding the Role of Resentment Dynamics from Other Places (Family, Work, and Friend Resentment Dynamics)

I believe that there can be little debate that resentment dynamics exist. As they are defined in this book, resentment dynamics are changes in the way that we feel and treat our partners that are triggered by anger at them. Are resentment dynamics limited to romantic relationships? I believe that the answer is no. Each of us has had resentment dynamics at work, within our families, and with our friends.

An important question to ask ourselves is, "Does the amount of resentment generated by our work, family, or friends affect our marital resentment dynamic?" Is it possible for us to be so tapped out emotionally from our other resentment dynamics that it affects our ability to forgive and tolerate the resentment generated by our primary relationship? Is it possible to have used so much of our ability to swallow our pride at work or in maintaining our relationships with our parents, siblings, children, or friends, that we don't have any tolerance or forgiveness left for the very relationship that gives us something back?

Is the world getting more difficult in general; playing a part in our general level of agitation or frustration?

Each relationship has resentments. Little resentments tend to be forgotten and forgiven over time. To the extent that we are generating things that our mates are resentful about, we tend to forgive their resentments a little easier. If we don't think that we are generating anything they should be resentful about, we are slower to forgive. If we don't forgive, if we can't or if it's too big, what do we do with it?

Does our pride keep us from approaching the people with whom we need to resolve our differences? Are we stubborn?

Being stubborn is both a good thing and a bad thing. Do we expect too much? Do we expect perfection? Can the frailties of human nature coexist with our expectations? Have our expectations (or what we require from a mate) become too extreme? Have talk shows, movies, and romance novels raised the bar so far on what we expect from a relationship that it simply can't be sustained for any extended period of time?

Resentment dynamics occur wherever we have long-term relationships; wherever we spend time with people and have expectations about their behavior. When we look at it this way, we realize that we have resentment dynamics at work and at home. We have resentment dynamics with our friends and with our family. We have resentment dynamics with our parents and our children. Few relationships are as unconditional as we would like them to be. The reality is that we are human and one of our frailties is that when our expectations are not met or when we feel used or taken for granted (hence work and family dynamics), we become angry. Are we always aware that some unmet need or disappointment has left us resentful or upset? Are we always aware that (much like a romantic relationship) our behaviors and attitudes toward those that offended us are changed in small or subtle ways? Do we necessarily see how we interact with them is different? That with friends, we are more distant, and with our parents, we are less likely to carve out time to come and see them or help with their care? Are our work resentments leading us to a downward spiral where we are less likely to stay late or work harder on projects if we feel discouraged, taken advantage of, or unappreciated? Are we just putting in our forty hours? Are we then the first person to leave the parking lot at the end of the day and the last to arrive; giving the impression to our superiors that we are just going through the motions and leading to a decreased chance of receiving a promotion or being given an important project?

As much as we would like this anger and resentment to just be forgotten and forgiven, most of the time it is not. It festers as our relationship resentments do; in its own basement. We have a work basement, a friend basement, and a family basement. For those of us with ex-wives and ex-husbands, we know from our own experience that the resentment generated from an ex often has a life of its own and can generate enough frustration and anger to disrupt even the happiest and most satisfying relationships.

Many of us also have a church resentment dynamic. Wherever our expectations are highest is where we tend to expect the most, and our places of worship are no exception. Show me a person who does not have some disappointment with their minister or religion and I will show you someone who lives in denial.

My point here is when we have resentments from other basements (whether that is our church basement, work basement, or parental basement); all of these conspire to affect the amount of junk accumulated in our collective basement. We need to realize that these other basements exist and perhaps work to resolve some of this resentment. The reason is simple: the amount of frustration we can tolerate is like a threshold. When we use up too much of our anger and frustration on our pastor or our boss, we have less tolerance for our mates.

Women's Expectations of Men

One of the things about women today is that they are finally in the position to be able to make decisions about whether they have to accept their mate's behavior or not. This has not always been the case. Women now no longer have to accept their mate's degree of emotional investment, their mate's ability to put off their own desires for the betterment of the family, their mates drinking, or emotional abusiveness. If he can do this, or if she can forgive enough, so much the better and there will probably be a long-term relationship. The natural extension of a man's inability to satisfy a woman's needs, however, inevitably leads to a withdrawing of her emotional investment in her mate and (more importantly) her sexual interest as well.

This leads to a cascade of behaviors and recriminations ending in alienation, frustration, and bitterness. Eighty percent of the time it is up to the man to make things right. **The being that created us does have a sense of humor.** Who, at least when we look at man in his most basic form, is less prepared to meet the emotional, physical, and spiritual needs of a family than a man? I can say this, I am a man.

This was fine a hundred years ago when men were actually *appreciated* for their natural traits. There was a time when risk-taking, physical strength, aggression, and "get the job done at whatever cost" attitude was valued. There was an author in the early 90s that said, to paraphrase: The easier the environment, the more female traits are valued, the harsher the environment, the more male traits are valued. When we look at the old west (or today's inner city), it's the male traits of aggression and risk-taking that were valued. In today's world, however, what most would consider an easier environment has none of these traits at all, but rather a different set of traits that are valued. In the modern workplace and in the modern family, a different set of abilities are needed and more appreciated. The ability to communicate well, to seek consensus, to listen to others, to value emotions (rather than see them as a liability), are the things that are appreciated. On the street, being emotional equals weak, which translates to being eaten. In a polite society (in today's world), being in touch with ones emotions, and maybe more importantly the emotional needs of others, is a huge advantage. This is something that many men (and in all honesty, some women) are only guessing at how to do. Yet, this is at the very root of staying intimately involved with our children and our mates. It is also the trait that I see in the very best employers, teachers, and coaches.

What this means for men is perhaps a wake-up call. Things need to change and they need to improve their skill set; particularly when it comes to their communication and emotional skills. Perhaps there is also a lesson here for women as well. Like all shifts in society, sometimes the pendulum swings too far out. Society changes too much and there needs to be a correction. This means a time to let the pendulum find a more balanced place in the middle of the continuum, rather than being at either end of the extreme. I mean that women's expectations of men went from very low (just that of being physical provider) to very high. In today's world, men are expected to be much more; perhaps more than they were ever prepared or designed to be. Today's woman expects her mate to:

1. 'Get' her
2. Be her best friend
3. Be romantic
4. Listen to her
5. Share his inner world with her
6. Communicate that he understands her inner world
7. Care for the children equally
8. Share the chores equally
9. And...Kill spiders

This may seem a rather lofty set of expectations. I laugh because I know a number of very intelligent and sophisticated men and frankly only half of them are up to this kind of task. My point is that just as men have to work harder to be the kind of men that women will need for the next century, women might need to lower their expectations if they want to increase their chances of finding happiness.

Figuring Out If One or Both of You Are Depressed?

One of the first things I usually do as a therapist is to determine whether one or both members of the couple is depressed, and if so, to what extent. If one of the members is depressed, it is important to work on their level of depression at the same time that we are working on the relationship. This may entail individual sessions with only one member of the couple as well as a consultation with a psychiatrist or primary care physician to rule out the need for antidepressant medication. Making a decision that will affect the rest of your life should be made with the utmost clarity. My experience is that if you are depressed, it is easy to make a mistake. If you are looking at making a major life decision, whether about a job change or a divorce, it makes sense to wait until you are centered or really emotionally healthy enough to make that decision. Decisions made in haste or out of desperation are oftentimes looked back on as being poor choices; made to reduce our pain or out of self-preservation rather than being what was truly in our own or our children's best interest.

Depression is not uncommon at this phase of the relationship because of the amount of stress put on a relationship and the amount of anxiety (think future that is uncertain) which naturally follows. If one of the individuals is depressed then it is important to also work on reducing the symptoms of depression along with resolving problems in the relationship. One without the other is futile. If you're getting more connected as a couple but still depressed and experiencing loss of interest in sex, looking sad, not feeling in love, etc., it is hard for the other to see the improvement and believe that the changes are really going to be integrated or real.

By the same token, if you work on reducing the symptoms of depression without encouraging the couple to resolve their differences, there is little likelihood of changing the initial dysfunctional dynamic that caused the emotional disconnection.

Where Does Depression Come From?

Current research suggests that there are three basic causes of depression. The first is the loss of a mother early in life. People who lose a mother when they are young tend to be depressed the rest of their lives. This is not an if-then correlation, meaning if you lose your mother early in life–then you will be depressed. What researchers are suspecting is that without the nurturance that mothers bring, and due to this trauma, certain structures of the brain may not fully develop. For many people, this translates to a low-grade depression for the rest of their lives. Most individuals who suffer from a low-grade depression are able to carry on a successful relationship, work, parent, etc. However, when stress levels go up, a low-grade depression can turn into a more significant depression.

The second most common cause of depression is the genetic predisposition to depression. This occurs when one or both of the client's parents also suffer from depression. What researchers suspect is that if a person with depression has children, there is a good chance that their children will not have a great number of receptor sites for serotonin; one of the main neurotransmitters associated with depression. When I counsel couples and it is clear that one of the parties is depressed, I frequently ask, "Is there any depression in your family?" Frequently I hear, "Oh yes, my mother is on Zoloft, my sister is on Wellbutrin," etc.

Lastly, researchers believe that one of the primary causes of depression is the extended presence of stress hormones in the human body and the brain in particular. When the human body is under stress, it produces stress hormones, adrenalin, cortisol, and a few other glucocorticoids. It seems our bodies have developed a stress response system to deal with periods of increased stress or fear. This system enables the body to increase the hormones we need to change our metabolic systems and increase the chances we will survive. However, these stress hormones are supposed to be in our system for a few hours (to get us up a tree and away from the bear that is chasing us), not a few months. Because when our bodies sense these hormones, we go into what is called the fight or flight mechanism. The fight or flight mechanism increases the flow of blood to our large muscles, our shoulders and our thighs, because we will need our large muscles to either fight what is stressing us or run from what is stressing us.

What is important to understand is that our bodies do not differentiate between the bear that is chasing us or problems with our wife or boss. All our body knows is that we are stressed and it responds in the way that it is programmed to respond. Due to needing blood to oxygenate the large muscles, the body has to divert blood away from somewhere else; in this case, the systems that are not needed for survival. This means that blood is diverted away from the penis since we do not need the penis to be engorged with blood, hence, robbing the body of the oxygen it needs. However, since we are being stressed by our deteriorating relationship with our spouse and not a bear, we wonder, "Why am I having difficulty getting and maintaining an erection?" We think, "Great, this is all I need."

The other system that seems to be the most affected by the presence of stress hormones is the digestive system. The digestive system requires a great deal of blood to process and absorb nutrients from our food. This starts with the blood needed by our stomachs to macerate or mash-up the foods we have just eaten. Now, most people who have been stressed know that they don't feel like eating because they have a ball in their stomachs. This is because we shut down the process of digestion in our stomachs and intestines as well. However, there are acids that continue to be pumped into our stomachs so we may develop an upset or nervous stomach, not feel like eating, or (in some cases) develop diarrhea.

When these stress hormones are in our system for a long period of time, a few months for example, it appears that they disrupt the delicate balance of neurotransmitters in the human brain. When this happens we become clinically depressed. Clinical depression is different from situational depression. Situational depression exists when there are time-limited circumstances which cause a state of sadness. When the condition changes, the feelings of sadness improve or go away altogether. This is different from clinical depression. When individuals are clinically depressed, there are changes in the brain chemistry that affect the person's ability to cope with life on a more substantial basis. And when a person is clinically depressed, they don't feel an improvement in their mood; even if the situation changes and is now the way they want it to be. It seems once these changes have affected the brain chemistry, it takes a while for those neurotransmitters to come back to normal levels.

Research also shows that when we become depressed, two specific areas of the brain are physically affected. This means that the cluster of cells that make up these two areas shrinks. They shrink because there is damage to the dendrites, a branch-like projection from a brain cell. The two areas that are most affected are the hippocampus and that portion of the brain called the reward center. The hippocampus is that portion of the brain that involves memory; specifically with transferring information from short-term to long-term memory. Because this structure shrinks, our memory is not as good. In fact, our memory stinks and we start to wonder if we are developing dementia.

The second portion of our brains that decrease in size is the area that is responsible for bringing us happiness and joy. We call it the reward center. Because it shrinks, however, the kinds of things that used to bring us joy and satisfaction–don't. This can be very troubling. The kinds of things that we used to enjoy, hobbies, interests, sex, even work, no longer bring us joy. So, we quit doing them. It happens in stages. Initially, we stop grooming and taking care of ourselves physically. We are fatigued and apathetic as well, so looking good, shaving, showering, and putting on makeup doesn't bring us pleasure. In this phase it is also common to find that we don't feel like cleaning the house or picking-up the usual clutter. This may also be one of the times where our partner's really start to see that we are depressed or cause even greater levels of resentment because we are not shouldering our portion of the home care load.

The last phase is the loss of interest in things that we really like to do. This is where people say, "I no longer feel like engaging in my hobbies, my gardening, reading, fishing, shopping, or exercising." I had a client recently say, "I knew I was depressed when I didn't feel like golfing or having sex." We start to withdraw from our old lives and become more isolated. Socializing and hanging out with friends doesn't sound like fun.

The good news is that as soon as we come out of our depression these clusters of cells return to normal size and we return to our old selves. Initially, it may feel like we have to force ourselves to engage in our old hobbies, going out with friends, mowing the lawn, etc. We really know we are better when these activities actually sound like fun again.

When we are depressed, we are in pain; the most exquisite emotional pain imaginable. People who are depressed not only lose interest in the kinds of things that they used to enjoy; they no longer have the interest or energy to engage in these activities. In essence, they sit on their couch and don't feel like doing anything. We call this apathy.

People who are depressed are also sensitive. This means not only are they sensitive about what others say, but they are sensitive to emotionally loaded situations as well. An example is when we see emotional commercials on TV and start to cry. When we are depressed, our emotions are very close to the surface. When we are depressed, we cry easily… We cry often.

When we are depressed, we become easily frustrated. Our frustration tolerance goes from taking a lot to get triggered to not needing much at all. Most people say they typically don't get mad easily. When we are depressed, it does not take much to frustrate or anger us. When we are depressed, it does not take much to frustrate or anger us. A professor of mine, Dr. Joe Oldz, once described it as being like this: when we become depressed we become hypersensitive to those around us. When we are not depressed and we go to a party and hear someone laughing, we don't think that they are laughing about us. When things are not going so well in our lives, we think, "They might be laughing at me." When we are clinically depressed and we go to a party and hear someone laugh, we are sure they are laughing at us. We are so sensitive that sometimes this borders on suspiciousness or paranoia.

This apathy and sensitivity can add a toxic element to a relationship if we do not recognize it for what it is. We may believe, inaccurately, that it is our marriage squeezing the lifeblood from us. This may be correct or it may be incorrect. In reality, we have stressed ourselves to the point of becoming depressed clinically, and these feelings are often an artifact of our depression rather than the actual relationship to which we attribute it.

So we lose interest in things, we cry at the drop of a hat, and we get upset easily. It is important to understand that being depressed is not like a light switch; either on or off, either you are depressed or you're not. Actually, there are gradients within the spectrum of depression ranging from a low-grade through severe. Sometimes we have good days and bad days. However, the more depressed individuals become, the more hopeless they become. Depressed individuals have a hard time seeing the end of the tunnel and only see how deep they are in the blackness and numbness of their depression. This may be the time to discuss the numbness that most people experience when they become depressed.

What I see when someone is depressed is this: it takes about all the energy they have to get up in the morning, shower and go to work. They have to make it look like they have their lives together, but they don't. They are on autopilot. They are going through the motions, and they can't tell if people know this or not. They are numb.

When we become depressed, we become deadened or insensitive to feelings. This means not only do we not feel happiness or joy, it also means that we don't feel pleasure or passion. My own experience with depression, as well as my experience as a therapist, has shown me that for the majority of people who have depression, when we are depressed we usually don't feel love, at least not romantic love. This is so significant; I feel the need to repeat it. When we are depressed, we don't feel love. We feel love for our children, but that is about it. We don't feel love toward our job, we don't feel love for golfing or hunting, and we sure don't feel love for our mates. *We don't feel romantic love.* We are numb.

If we are unhappy and we don't feel like we love our mates, the natural extension of this is to either find something that does make us feel alive or to get out of the relationship that is sucking us dry and leaving us so unhappy.

When we are this depressed, it is normal to start to get desperate. We think that if this relationship is making us depressed, we need to find something that will make us feel again. People hate feeling numb. This sets us up to use some person, some thing, or some activity as medicine. We need relief from our pain.

As we become more desperate, we start to go into a self-preservation mode. After an individual has started to become depressed, they often stop caring about working on the relationship, and frankly, they are becoming a slave to their depression. As with all people who are depressed they become apathetic and lose the energy to work on things. Due to this, they start to wonder if they are better off lonely or miserable.

Depression occurs over a continuum; from mildly sad to extremely depressed. I usually ask people to rank their mood on a scale of 1-10 with 10 being extremely depressed. Five is a sense of, "I am not really happy or sad, I am just here." This is what I consider a low-grade depression, where you're not exactly sad but you rarely feel happiness either. (One would be, "I have never been happier.") Individuals who score over about an 8 on the mood scale start to experience something that the other individuals don't. Once people reach a certain degree of depression they often start to experience thoughts like, "Is this a life worth living?" Many make statements like, "I don't plan on killing myself but I have thoughts of, wouldn't my family be better off without me?" or "If I have to live the rest of my life feeling like this, I would rather save myself the trouble." Some people say, "I don't actually have plans to commit suicide, but if I got cancer or someone crossed the median and killed me that wouldn't be so bad." These thoughts are normal; especially in individuals who are experiencing severe clinical depression. Very few people who reach this point ever develop a plan to actually attempt to take their life. If they do reach that point, they need to contact their primary care physician or therapist and arrange to be hospitalized for a brief period so that they don't harm themselves.

The thing about getting to this point is that one starts to ask themselves, "If I am this depressed and living with my spouse seems to be causing the sadness, am I better off taking my life or getting out of the relationship to at least be some use to somebody else?" In other words, our depression motivates us into action. Despite our lack of energy for almost any other activity, when we are depressed we are motivated to leave our spouse; if only to save our lives.

Making Decisions When Depressed

There are a lot of blind spots when we are depressed. Blind spots mean things we just can't see when we are depressed. But if we are blind to them, how can we know that they exist? This is where a therapist can help. Are things as bad as they appear financially or with our relationship? What is our role in this? What are all of my options?

We are blinded by our pain and discomfort when we are depressed. We just want out; we just want relief from our pain. We become desperate to end it. If it is the job's fault, we want to quit. If it is the relationship's fault, we want a divorce.

The thing I tell my clients is that they need to be as emotionally centered as possible before they start to make any life-changing plans. You can't go back and take a mulligan or change your mind if you make a decision and then decide a year later (after coming out of the depression) that perhaps you were hasty, should have perhaps stayed in the marriage, worked harder on a plan, or not quit your job. Making life-changing decisions when you are depressed is a bad idea. What I tell my clients is "Let's get you out of this depression first. If you still want to quit your job or get a divorce in three months, then I will support you." In eighty percent of the cases, once a person starts to come out of their depression and develops some hope for a future, they thank me for not letting them be too hasty when it came to making decisions regarding their future.

Is There Something Else Going On In Our Partner's Life?

Sometimes we think that we have found the perfect partner. They are everything that we have been looking for: they are attractive, smart, easygoing, and a good match. They enjoy the same things that we do, plus they enjoy sex! Great, we beat the odds. Things go on for a period of time and we eventually get married and have kids or integrate our children and our lives into their family and their life.

Then something starts to happen. The look changes in their eyes. There is a distance. They seem preoccupied. We no longer feel like we are their top priority. It seems like their thoughts are on something else. They may seem edgy or easily frustrated. What was once an interest in physical intimacy now ends up being a source of frustration. We start to feel more distant and frustrated. We start to grow resentful. Were we misled somehow? We ask, "Was this a bait and switch?" We start to wonder, "Is the honeymoon over?" We start to develop a resentment dynamic.

Before you throw the towel in or start to back away emotionally, perhaps you should ask yourself some questions. Is there something going on in your partner's life? Are they stressed? Are they (or one of their children) having health problems? Do they like their job? Are they depressed? Are they going through a period of PMS?

Perhaps this is a temporary condition that is an artifact of how stressed they are at work or in their personal life. Perhaps this is the time to show them how mature and patient you can be. Our partners need to hear, "Don't worry, we will get through this." They need to know that you are not going to bolt just because you are not getting the amount of sex that you used to get or because they seem preoccupied.

Before you make any major decisions, perhaps you should ask yourself some more questions. Am I being unrealistic about my expectations? Isn't it natural for the frequency of sex to decrease? As we grow more comfortable with each other, isn't it normal for us to use our partner as the one who is safe enough to blowup at? The one we can vent our frustrations on? We certainly can't vent these on our co-workers or our boss. My experience is that most of the time there are troughs and crests within every relationship. There are times when financially, emotionally, and stress wise, things are going well. We feel connected to our mates at an even deeper level than we thought possible. This is good because it needs to tide us over during that which is probably coming, a period of instability. Perhaps a period of financial or family stress or perhaps a child who has historically been well behaved and quick to please is starting to test the boundaries of your world (and your patience).

These times rarely last, and yet they can feel like they go on forever. These periods test relationships as well; especially if there are two different parenting styles or expectations. But children grow up and move away, bosses come and go, and financial responsibilities become more manageable. Nothing lasts forever. When things even out and stress levels subside, you will be glad that you didn't flee and start over on your own.

We Are More Like Others Than We Realize

It is said in psychology, "There are parts of us that are like no other person, there are parts of us that are like some other people, and there are parts of us that are like all other people." The mistake that we often make is in believing that the part of us that is unique is big and that we are special, unique, and unlike any other individual. Actually, that part of us that is special or unique only to us is smaller than most people think. Most of us actually share many of the same experiences with others and we tend to respond to situations in similar ways. That is why so many people will find this book helpful. My observations will probably resonate with most of you. Not only the question of what happens to unresolved issues and how that affects your level of intimacy with your partner, but also the stages that you went through when growing alienated from them. Rather than see this as a negative thing and take away the sense that, "I am not as special as I used to think"; I would choose to see it as, "I am sharing this most human of experiences. I guess it must be a normal response."

How Should You Confront Your Partner On Their Behavior?

Do emotional pleas for behavior change work? If I cry and tell my partner how angry I am at their behavior, will they change? If I scream and yell, is this going to get their attention and make them take me seriously? Actually both of these strategies can work. However, if you are still reading this book, chances are that they haven't. Chances are that you have already tried these approaches without success. Now what do you do? What do you do when yelling and crying don't work to get your partner to change their behavior?

As I said before, the average woman leaves her husband six times before she actually leaves him for good. I am not sure how many times the average husband leaves his wife before *he* actually leaves for good. The point is that rarely do people succeed in leaving their mate on the first try. They are usually angry and frustrated enough to give it a shot, but they get pulled back. Or, they realize they don't have the resources to survive without their partner's help. Sometimes they get a guilt induction from their parents or their children and they relent and move back. Oftentimes the reason that people come back is that they are told, "I will change. I know I can." They want to believe that their partner, whom at some level they still care for, is able to be the person they need; a grown adult with an eye toward the best interest of their family. They need to know that they made a good choice in who they married. Certainly, they would grow up over time, right? What happens eighty percent of the time is that things are, in fact, better for a period of time, sometimes a month, sometimes longer. More often than not, however, they revert back to their previous behaviors. The basement is getting smellier and smellier; filled with years of unresolved issues and the resentment that they bring. It doesn't take much to tap into our reservoir of resentment. We overreact to even the smallest broach of our trust. We tell ourselves, "I should never have taken them back."

Women frequently ask, "How do you know when you are finally ready to move on, to move out?" What I tell them is, "Oh, you will know." It is difficult to explain to someone how they will feel when they are truly ready to move on, when they are done emotionally, when they don't care anymore. There is no equation, no way to really know consistently from one person to another how much it will take to bring them to this place. Each person is different. Some call it reaching the bottom. The reality is some people don't have a bottom. Much like an alcoholic who has to get so disgusted with their own behavior that they finally quit drinking, people in relationships have to reach a point where they are done emotionally. But much like the alcoholic, some never reach their bottom and drink themselves to death. Some, however, realize that they need to change only when their doctor says they have destroyed their liver and have six months to live. Some quit when they get their third drunk driving ticket and have to go to prison. *And some quit when their wives say they are going to leave them. No yelling, no screaming. In a quiet voice that says they are serious this time. The look in someone's eyes often speaks volumes about the seriousness and sincerity of the warning.*

Perhaps you are the individual who has left several times and then ultimately moved back in. You have threatened and threatened and now feel that your words no longer have any weight. You have backed off your threats so many times that they are no longer taken seriously. Is your partner saying under their breath, "You're not leaving." We leveraged divorce or at least threatened it. Sometimes we have had our bluff called so many times that we wonder ourselves if we have the strength to actually do it; to actually move out and take our chances on our own. If this is you, I am trying to normalize this behavior. I am telling you that it is perfectly normal. In fact, it is the way it is done. However, the important point is not in the leaving; it is in the how do I stay? How do you know that you did everything that you could to try and work things out? Everyone knows that if you eventually leave, you want to know that you exhausted every avenue of reconciliation; leveraged every bit of emotional connection that you had to get your partner to change his or her behavior. You left no cards on the table.

There is no perfect way to get your partner to take you seriously. I think it is important, however, to have them understand how close you are to finally leaving.. The reason it is important is that you can actually wait too long and be ready to leave without having actually given your partner a chance to make the changes you need.

It is important to understand that I am not encouraging wives to leave their husbands or husbands to leave their wives. I am simply stating all of the options that need to be understood when making decisions that have to do with one's long-term plans.

If, however, you have given them the opportunity to be the person you need and there is still no improvement, then perhaps you **do** need to take your time, give them a final ultimatum, and make plans to move out. How will they know that you are serious? Your partner will know when you do this:

1. When you have spoken to an attorney about your options and how much you will get from your spouse, or how much you will have to pay to your spouse (and you are OK with it). You have discussed with your attorney whether you will have to leave the home or if you have options to stay in it. If you have children, you know what the chances are that you will get custody or partial custody and have made peace with this arrangement.

2. When you have put money aside or saved money, or you have approached your support network (meaning either family or friends) about borrowing money to start divorce proceedings and to provide enough to survive financially; at least until you are stable enough independently.

3. You have looked at alternate housing and realistically understand what you can afford. The more specifically you can say that you have looked, the more serious you will be seen. If you say, "I have found an apartment and I am on the waiting list," this is taken more seriously than, "I know I can afford an apartment."

When you approach your mate after having successfully done these three things (talked to a lawyer, gotten together the resources, and looked at houses or apartments), then they know that you are serious about leaving them. This also gives you a different peace of mind, a different confidence.

One of the things that so often keep people from leaving a relationship is what I refer to as a future that is uncertain. "Will I be able to afford it?" "Will I have to change my standard of living?" "Will I be able to see the children as much?" When these issues have been addressed and you have gotten hard data, you know how much you will have per month to spend on housing and groceries; you know what kind of house or apartment you will have to live in for a while. You have made peace with perhaps not having the children every day. Then your future is not so uncertain. This changes the way you approach someone. It no longer has an air of a threat to it. You can say with some confidence, "I have talked to a lawyer, I have looked at some apartments, and I have found one I like." This is different than when you move out after a fight. If your partner does not change their behavior after this confrontation, *they probably aren't going to.*

Chapter Seventeen

CLOSING THOUGHTS

One of the things I tell my clients is that you can't take a dead body to the Mayo Clinic and expect them to resurrect it. If the relationship is dead, if there is nothing but indifference and apathy, the reality is that there is nothing you can do with such relationships other than to negotiate a civil end.

Most couples say that initially there was a flame, then it started to flicker, and then it became a dying ember. But oftentimes we are so alienated from our partners and so disconnected from them that we don't know if what we have is a smoldering ember waiting to be fanned or a dead chunk of coal. What if there is an ember there? What if you were to fan this ember or put some energy back into the relationship? What would happen? What if you were able to resolve your issues and no longer dump issues down in the basement? What would happen to that flame? Are you really such a poor match? Or rather, as I see much more frequently, couples that are not inherently a bad match, but they simply grew apart due to the loss of intimacy between them.

Couples ask themselves, "Would the laughing come back? Would the sex come back? Would the teasing or play come back?" These are the very best parts of relationships and couples naturally wonder if the best years, those at the early part of their relationship, can ever be restored. They ask me, "Can this come back?" And the answer is an enthusiastic yes, absolutely! These things come back, the sense of closeness, the sense of being friends, and the sex.. The sense of being in love comes back. But it takes a lot of energy and you have to learn the rules of arguing in a civil manner and how to get your point across without hurting the other person. You have to learn to pick your battles and most importantly, you have to learn how to stay on topic and focus on the issue you were discussing all the way until you get closure.

The caveat is that relationships can be restored as long as they are not dead. It is so encouraging for me as a therapist to see couples come back after working on their relationship for five or six weeks and see the changes in them. You can see a difference almost every week in the way they look at each other and how close they sit to each other. Things like smiling at each other come back and they are touching or holding hands again. What a difference from the two alienated people that sat across from me only a month ago. It is so wonderful to have them say to me "We have never felt this connected, this happy." We felt this way when we first started to date, but it was artificial, it was chemical, it was infatuation. This is different. This is real love, I know who you are, I see your faults, I see your warts, I know those parts of you that are broken. We see each other not through the goggles of infatuation but in a more realistic way, a way that says, with all your humanness, I still love you. That love that we initially felt for each other really is there. We didn't believe it for a while, but we are made for each other.

This is how it is when a couple appreciates how alike they are and how fortunate they are to have worked through their differences. This is now a mature love, a mature relationship. Not an artificial, chemically induced trance, but a real relationship that has been exposed to the stresses of modern life and has survived. Couples realize they have gone to the precipice, looked over, and realized that they don't want that. They don't want to breakup. This is a different relationship. As I said earlier, some things are best revealed in their absence. Sometimes, it is only in losing something or almost losing something that we realize how important it is to us.

The path to a satisfying marriage is a difficult one. To make this voyage, one must possess the tools in one's toolbox to make such a journey. It's not just knowing how to use conflict management skills or improving communication. It is not just learning how to tolerate uncomfortable emotions between you and your spouse or understanding your role in how the situation got the way it is. Each of these insights fulfills one of the tools needed to build a good marriage. Each of these represents a tool in your collective toolbox.

For me, the key to a good marriage is learning how to reach a state of intimacy. Not a "fall in love" induced trance, but a real relationship based on trust and respect. A relationship that has been exposed to the light of day, to the other's faults, and still remains. Finding this state of intimacy is difficult. Maintaining this state of connectedness is even more difficult.

There are so many threats to relationships today. Threats like selfishness, substance abuse, and the opportunity to find alternative relationships so easily on the Internet.

Building a satisfying long-term relationship means working on ourselves first; getting our own house in order. We as individuals have to understand the buttons that make us angry, our character faults, dishonesty, ego, needing to be in control, and talking to our mates disrespectfully. If we want to win the prize of a long-term, monogamous, satisfying relationship, we have to be able to look in our own mirror.

Ultimately, the key to a good relationship is learning to resolve your differences. The key to that is to be able to compromise or negotiate an agreement that both individuals can live with (and keep). This is something I can bring to your awareness, but can't teach you to do. Compromising is about trust, about trusting your partner to return the favor. It is about giving in a little. It is about ego, about not having to always have your way and seeing your partner's best interest instead of yours for the sake of the relationship. It is about being flexible versus rigid or having to always have your way. These things I can't teach. These are issues of maturity and wisdom.